viva!
ZAPPA

CRéDitS

First published © 1985 Calmann-Levy, Paris.
This edition © Copyright 1986 Omnibus Press
(A Division of Book Sales Limited)
French to English Translation by Matthew Screech
Edited by Chris Charlesworth
Art Direction by Paul Alessandrini
Book Designed by Philippe Huart, Pearl Cholley, Jim Little (UK)
Co-ordinated by Lynda Hassett

ISBN 0.7119.0821.4
Order No. OP 43702

Exclusive distributors:
Book Sales Limited
78 Newman Street, London W1P 3LA, UK.

Music Sales Corporation
24 East 22nd Street, New York,
NY 10010, USA.

Omnibus Press
GPO Box 3304, Sydney,
NSW 2001, Australia.

To the Music Trade only:
Music Sales Limited
78 Newman Street, London W1P 3LA, UK.

Picture credits: Bizarre Records (122, 16/1, 19), CBS Records (30,
35, 41, 74, 78, 107), Discreet Records (68), Claude Gassian (4, 20,
22, 29, 34, 40, 49, 57, 69/1, 69/2, 70, 95, 108, 109), Art Kane (17),
Bernard Leloup (44/45), Pathe Marconi (21, 24, 37, 58, 80, 82, 100,
119), Christian Rose (6, 13, 26, 27, 32, 42, 46/1, 47, 51, 52/2, 54, 116),
Guido Harari (33, 38, 46/2, 48, 52, 77, 91, 93, 97, 104, 112, 114),
Lynn Goldsmith (60, 73, 75, 76), Verve Records (11, 62, 12/1, 62),
Bruce Webber (16, 18, 46, 67, 84), Zappa Records (120, 127), Unknown
(8, 9, 10, 14, 15, 79, 86/1, 86/2, 101, 124, 126).

The author thanks Phillippe Paringaux (US tour photographer), Jacques
Hubert, Mick Safont, P. Moreau, B. Gueffier, P. Renaud, Nicole
Hollington, Francoise Serre, Gilles Petard and J.-N. Ogouz.

Typeset by floppy disc by Serious Software.
Printed in Scotland by Scotprint Limited, Musselburgh.

ZAPPA!

DOMINIQUE CHEVALIER

Omnibus Press

London/New York/Sydney/Cologne

CÖNteNTS

1

iNTERCÖNtiNENTAL

abSURdiTies

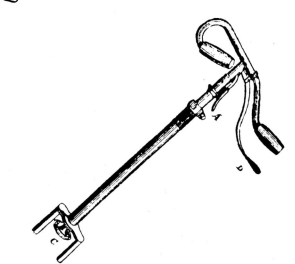

America Drinks And Goes Home

There's not much to Cucamonga. Just a few shops, bars, a school and a church. But it was in this sleepy little town that the Frank Zappa story began. One day in the early '60s, a young guitarist from San Diego bought a recording studio at 8040 Archibald Avenue with money earned from composing the music to a low budget film. But no sooner was Studio Z born than trouble began. A cop who used to hang around the bars where Zappa occasionally appeared asked him to produce a tape that would help train the San Bernadino Vice Squad. Another insisted that the tapes should be a bit 'hot'.

Zappa obliged by bouncing around with one of his girlfriends, groaning and grunting into a microphone. But once the laughter had been wiped off the tape, the cops changed their tune and raided the studio, confiscated the equipment and arrested Zappa for 'conspiracy to propagate pornography, lust and lascivious attitudes'.

He got three years probation (which exempted him from military service) and was 'forbidden to frequent a woman less than 21 years old, unless in the presence of a responsible adult'. "It was the most absurd thing that has ever happened to me", Zappa said later.

This unlikely episode is somehow typical of the adventures that would dog Francis Vincent Zappa throughout his career.

He was born in Baltimore, Maryland, on December 21, 1940. His father, Francis Vincent Zappa senior, is a scientist with a degree from the University of Chapell Hill, North Carolina, who worked at various times as an analyst, engineer and metallurgist at the Lockheed and Corvair aircraft corporations. In 1950, he got a job at the naval school in Monterey, and Mr and Mrs Zappa took their family, which also included Frank's brothers and sister, Bob Carl and Candy, there. They stayed three years before continuing their travel to Pomona, then to San Diego, where Mr Zappa worked on Atlas Missiles in Lancaster, a base famous today for the space shuttle.

These constant changes influenced young Frank's imagination in important ways and were to resurface in his project for a rock opera 'I Was A Teenage Maltshop'. After a few disastrous attempts at mastering chemistry, music became his main interest. In 1951, at the age of twelve, he persuaded his parents to buy him a small drum set and spent most of his time practising. He joined a school group, proudly announcing to his father that he was, "going to earn a million dollars." Frank senior did not laugh at this. "I believed what he said, I always took him seriously, he was a serious boy," he said later.

Frank was equally aware of his potential, and in this he was not alone. At school, a master called Mr Tosi (to whom 'Freak Out' is dedicated) regarded him as a very independent character who, though not always hard working, was capable of the highest achievements in areas that interested him, and Frank was already won over by music.

When he was thirteen, Frank read an article in *Look* magazine about record dealer Sam Goody. It praised the wide range of

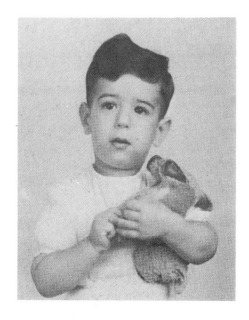

music that could be found in his store and gave as an example an obscure record called 'Ionisation, The Complete Works of Edgar Varèse Volume One'. After a long and frustrating search, Frank found a scratched demonstration copy and, to his mother's horror, played it over and over again on the family gramophone. On his fifteenth birthday Frank used the $5 he was given to make a long distance call to Varèse. He started composing at about this time and 'Mice', a piece for percussion, is one of these early efforts.

At eighteen, while visiting his aunt Mary in Baltimore, Frank tried to contact his idol Varèse again, but he had just left for Europe. After this disappointment he returned to California and enrolled at Antelope Valley Junior College, where he only stayed for one term, as the Zappas left for Claremont.

Frank soon left home to live in a small flat in Echo Park. He helped his English teacher, who was writing a low budget western called *Run Home Slow*, by composing a score for the soundtrack. These were lean times, and after returning to his family for a while, he enrolled for a course in harmony at Chaffee Junior College, Alta Loma, more to meet girls than to learn. Frank's formal education eneded with a final composition course in Pomona.

At about this time Frank met his first wife, Kay. Their marriage was to last five years. At first Kay worked at the National Bank of Ontario to pay the rent and other necessities while Frank played rhythm and blues on the cocktail bar circuit, work which probably inspired songs such as 'America Drinks And Goes Home'. He also found a job as artistic director at a firm that made greetings cards, and during this brush with commercial reality learnt the first principles of marketing. In 1960 he wrote the score for a fifth-rate film called *The World's Greatest Sinner* and passed through a series of brief jobs and short-lived groups until 1963 when *Run Home Slow* resurfaced starring Mercedes Macambridge. With the money he earned from this, Frank bought his own studio and his first quality guitar, an instrument he began learning at eighteen.

Frank soon found himself joining a variety of musical characters in bands that were continually forming and splitting up. Among them were The Soots (with Don Vliet, later Captain Beefheart) and The Muthers (with Paul Woods and Les Papp), who played in bars full of Mexican workmen like The Sinners And Saints in Ontario (California). Frank also joined The Soul Giants with Roy Estrada, Ray Collins and Jim Black.

On Mother's Day evening, 1964, they decided to change their name. From now on they would be called The Mothers.

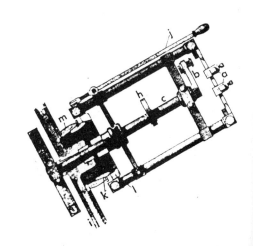

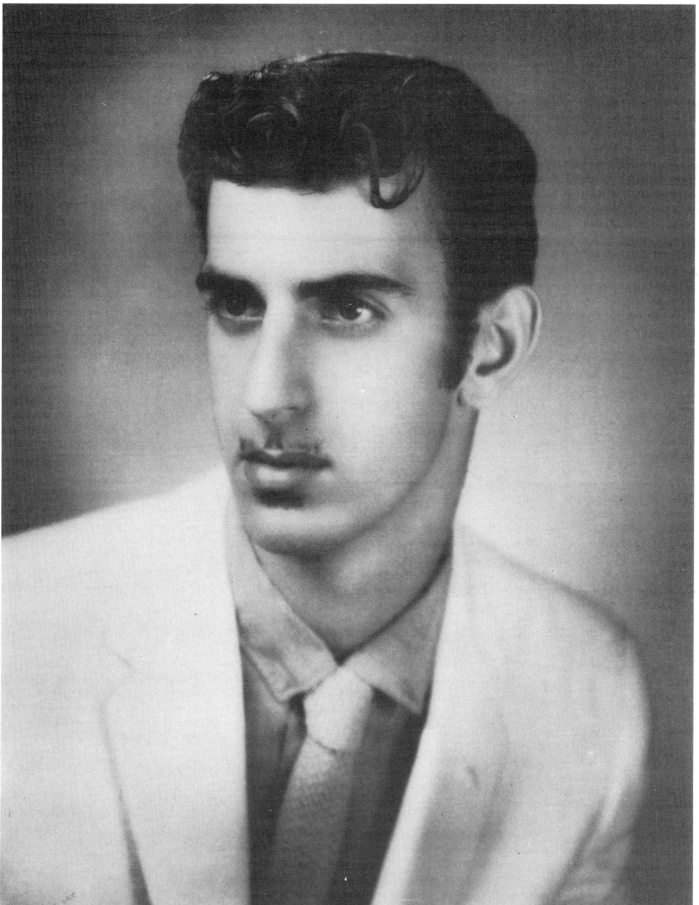

Mondo Holywood 1965

This small-time work continued for a while and among the musicians who passed through The Mothers were Henry Vestine (later of Canned Heat), Jim Guercio (who has since produced Chicago), Van Dyke Parks, Dr John and Jim Fielder. It was a time when the little world of Hollywood was full of contradictions. Shaken by recent clashes with the forces of law and order, the city of showbiz became host to a buzzing fringe culture, and at the centre of this little world sat Vito, a sculptor-dancer remarkable for catalyzing the Los Angeles 'freak' scene. Vito, king of the bizarre, was visited by the likes of Allen Ginsberg, Donovan and Lenny Bruce, and among his wide circle of friends was one Carl Franzoni.

Carl had seen Zappa playing in various bars, and introduced him to the high and hip places of L.A. freakdom. It was at a documentary film presentation on the freaks' extravaganzas that Zappa met his future manager, Herb Cohen.

He also made an important friend in Pamela Zarubica. Pamela was finishing her studies and had little interest in rock, but she knew everybody: Phil Spector, Tim Hardin, John Densmore and Jim Morrison of the Doors, Zal Yanovsky of The Lovin' Spoonful and John Judnick who knew Lenny Bruce, and they all made contact with Zappa. Pamela contemplated her network of acquaintances with a healthy indifference to the vanities and vainglories of their recently acquired celebrity – "That Jim Morrison sure was a drag, always play acting and making everybody listen to his poems!"

Pamela later became a 'Surrogate Mother' in the guise of the famous Suzy Creamcheese. She and Frank took a house at 8404 Kirkwood while she was finishing school and simultaneously working as week-end secretary at the Whiskey-A-Gogo. One night at the Whiskey she met Gail Sloatman, the daughter of a scientist with the U.S. Navy. Born on January 1, 1945, Gail had just returned from a stay in England and New York. One day Pamela took her to the airport to meet Frank returning from playing in Texas. It was a fateful encounter for Gail would soon become his permanent companion, the mother of Dweezil, Moon Unit, Ahmet Rhodan and Diva. It was soon after they met that Pamela left for Europe and Gail moved in with Frank at Kirkwood.

In November 1965 Tom Wilson, who had just started working for MGM Records after producing Bob Dylan for Columbia, happened across The Mothers playing at the Whiskey-A-Gogo. He offered them a contract and a recording budget of $21,000, a considerable sum for a totally unknown group in 1965.

The first Mothers' album would be a double LP containing several very long pieces that could not be instantly transformed into likely hit singles with which to promote it. A precedent was being set which, in time, would alter the entire framework of the record industry.

The music on '*Freak Out*', rock's first concept album, was recorded between November 1965 and January 1966. Released in August, 1966, it tells of the riots in the L.A. black ghetto Watts, Suzy Creamcheese and her associates, Carl Franzoni, assorted freaks and much more. The studio techniques that Zappa had learned at Studio Z both impressed and worried the sound engineers.

Defying convention the recording sessions took on the air of spontaneous happenings as Zappa, already confident of what he was doing, stood on a rostrum with a baton in hand and conducted orgies of sound such as '*Help I'm A Rock!*'

Pigs And Repugnants

Hot on the heels of '*Freak Out*', The Mothers recorded a second album, '*Absolutely Free*', the week before Thanksgiving 1966 in less than twenty four hours at TTG studios in L.A. It was remixed a few weeks later in less than thirty six hours, an impressive feat considering the quality of sound and its musical complexity. The budget of $11,000 was ridiculously low.

In 1966 there was no new album more complex than '*Absolutely Free*', except perhaps George Martin and The Beatles' efforts in different directions. With constant semi-parodies, cross-references to different kinds of music and abrupt changes of tempo, '*Absolutely Free*' is an artful collage, a page of contemporary history, a rock oratorio. It also captures on vinyl much of the craziness of The Mothers' shows at the Garrick Theater, New York.

The Garrick is on Bleeker Street in Greenwich Village and nearby, in the basement of the Café-A-Gogo, both The Fugs and Jimi Hendrix were performing at about the same time. The Mothers' show, titled '*Pigs And Repugnants*', was a resounding success, and the band stayed for six months, playing two shows a night, six nights a week. Anything might happen, depending on the mood and on new arrivals like Don Preston and Bunk Gardner.

Many evenings gave rise to memorable incidents. One night a party of uniformed marines came in, and Zappa persuaded them to mime the act of killing. The audience could not believe their eyes as the furious marines mutilated a doll and insulted the army, all against a background of free jazz. A black man at the front, just home from Vietnam, broke down in tears and spoke of deserting. The show was often grotesque or sexual, but a fascinated audience always lapped it up.

F.Z, Elliot Ingber, Ray Collins, Jimmy Carl Black, Roy Estrada, 1966.

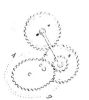

PUBLISHED WHEN WE CAN AFFORD IT
MOSTLY
FOR
FUN

FREAK OUT!
official news of M.O.I.

Billy Mundi, Roy Estrada, Ray Collins, Don Preston, Jimmy Carl Black, Bunk Gardner, F.Z, 1967.

Ray Collins, Jimmy Carl Black, F.Z, Art Tripp, Roy Estrada, Bunk Gardner, Don Preston, James Motorhead Sherwood, Ian Underwood, 1968.

The Mothers stayed at the Garrick until the start of 1967 and apart from brief visits to Canada and L.A., Zappa took advantage of his spell in New York to produce four albums: 'Lumpy Gravy', 'We're Only In It For The Money', 'Uncle Meat' and Cruising With Ruben And The Jets'. Originally 'Lumpy Gravy' was to appear on Capitol who wanted Zappa to record what they termed 'serious music'. His contract with Verve stipulated that he was a producer, so Frank decided he could make a record for Capitol as a composer and arranger.

This he did, and 'Lumpy Gravy' was recorded in less than eleven days with some of the best studio musicians available. But Verve blocked the project and it was eleven months before the record was finally released with contributions by The Mothers.

In February 1967, early rumblings of what some called the 'New American Culture' could be heard: anti-Vietnam war demonstrations, sexual rebellion, wider use of psychedelic drugs, flower power, and pop music's eruption into the media. Early records by unknown groups had laid the foundations for the pop's revolution, but Frank Zappa realised immediately where the future lay. 'We're Only In It For The Money' was originally to be called 'Our Man In Nirvana', a skilful blend of The Mothers' music and Lenny Bruce's lyrics, to be released in September, but after The Beatles made a vast cultural impression with 'Sergeant Pepper', he realised the full extent of this new culture's potential.

The whole groovy flower power scene would produce the pop idols of tomorrow, while the so-called sexual and psychedelic revolution would soon be challenged by the media and the political powers. So Zappa changed his plans and hired a young graphic artist, Calvin Schenkel, to parody The Beatles' sleeve. Zappa and Schenkel substituted female transvestite clothes for The Beatles' military uniforms, and replaced the flowers with carrots and sliced water melons. Paul McCartney for one, was not amused, and the album's release was delayed until the end of the year, but 'We're Only In It For The Money' established Zappa as both a force to be reckoned with on the rock scene and as a sharp social critic.

Jefferson Airplane wanted him to produce their LP 'After Bathing At Baxters', Eric Clapton dropped round to play guitar, and Jimi Hendrix, who borrowed Frank's wah-wah pedals back at the Garrick Theater, posed for the inner sleeve. Clapton also contributed some incomprehensible vocals on one track, offering a fair impersonation of someone who is thoroughly stoned.

But record company trouble loomed. MGM had yet to pay royalties on the first four albums and had censored words it found unsuitable on later pressings. So Zappa decided to take full responsibility for producing his own music, and left Tom Wilson to form Bizarre Productions and Straight Records. The move was to give rise to albums that were less controversial but more musically oriented: 'Uncle Meat' and 'Ruben And The Jets' among others.

In January 1968, Zappa spent almost 180 hours in Apostolic Studios, New York, where he simultaneously recorded two albums while working on a film of 'Uncle Meat'. The script was written during the recording sessions, and while the group recorded one track Zappa sat in the sound engineer's room composing music for the next one. As he said on the sleeve, the lyrics were mostly a selection of dreams, syllables and in-jokes, all 'scientifically prepared'.

'Ruben And The Jets' was finished while 'Uncle Meat' was still in preparation, with Jimmy Carl Black, Ray Collins, Roy Estrada, Jim Sherwood, Ian Underwood and new drummer Art Tripp III. 'Ruben And The Jets' shows Zappa's fondness for the doo-wop/R&B style of fifties vocal groups. It contains all the favourite clichés plus superbly cretinous lyrics, and was released in December 1968 to general indifference, although John Lennon and George Harrison sent a cable to Zappa expressing their admiration.

It was certainly a bold move to release a vocal R&B album at the height of the psychedelic era, and it remains an early indicator of the early '70s pop-rock revival.

This is an Italian salute.

Indicates to play in 7/8 on cue.

The Brooklyn cue for "I forgot my part"; this indicates that everybody is supposed to stop playing and walk around the stage looking as worried as possible, rubbing their forehead and looking like they haven't got the faintest idea of what they are supposed to do during the section. Then, they abruptly come back in on cue.

Electrified Boogies

With '*Uncle Meat*' Zappa moved away from rock-theatre towards a new kind of electric chamber music. Meticulous care was taken over the mixing, and overdubbing was pushed to its limits – up to forty tracks on the middle section of '*Dog Breath*'. The music contained more brass, woodwind and percussion, and synthesisers appeared for the first time. '*Uncle Meat*' was recorded between October '67 and February '68, and was originally to be a triple album titled '*No Commercial Potential*'.

The music is at times influenced by Conlon Nancarrow, and the band comprised eight or nine members, about twice the size of most rock groups. The music was more complex, and some of the band, particularly Jimmy Carl Black and Jim Sherwood, found it harder to play. Although Ian Underwood and Art Tripp could pick it up easily enough, Zappa was forced to spend more and more time making the others practise their parts, which was exhausting, especially as the band was always on tour. To overcome the problem he invented a unique sign-language, a mixture of conducting and miming to change the flow of the music as he directed his gestures or grimaces at one musician or another.

Like a ringmaster in a modern musical circus, he shaped the improvised and previously prepared sections from his imaginary rostrum, which also enabled him to judge the playing from a critical distance and to become the first spectator of his own music.

The Electric Chamber Orchestra

In 1968 and 1969 The Mothers toured the U.S. and Europe almost without a break, and the band, pushed to its limits by Zappa, was both physically and financially exhausted. While trendies played acid-rock, Zappa's band, with its numerous wind instruments, two keyboards, two percussionists, and often a violin and a second guitar, was unique.

This electric chamber orchestra travelled all over the place, playing a weird sort of music which consisted increasingly of free jazz and neo-classical contemporary music. It was finally disbanded at the door of its 'two hundredth motel' in August 1969.

Two albums, '*Weasels Ripped My Flesh*' and '*Burnt Weeny Sandwich*' came from this period. The latter, appropriately titled, consists of complex instrumental music sandwiched between two chirpy pop songs. Was it an attempt to introduce the public to music closer to Stravinsky and Satie than to The Doors by including two samples of typical radio playlist material? '*Holiday In Berlin*' on side one, was inspired by the extreme left-wing unrest in Berlin in September 1968.

The far-leftists, looking for a new leader to follow Rudi Dutschke, saw Zappa as a figurehead or guru and asked him to go with them to burn a government building, which he refused to do, "We have come to play music" was Frank's reaction. The extremists immediately accused Frank of being a Nazi and chanted "Mother of Reaction". The concert audience stormed the stage as the band, fearful of damage, hastily packed up their instruments. The hall was in uproar, and quickly degenerated into a grotesque re-run of the Paris student riots in May '68.

'Weasels Ripped My Flesh', closer to Eric Dolphy and free jazz, came out in 1970. Zappa had already recorded 'Hot Rats' between August and September 1969, in a 16-track studio. This album is primarily a collaboration with Ian Underwood. The pair play most of the instruments, along with various jazz musicians and other specialists including John Guerin, Jean Luc Ponty, Don 'Sugarcane' Harris, Captain Beefheart, Max Bennett and Shuggy Otis, son of Johnny Otis.

With 'Hot Rats', one of his most successful albums, Zappa completed his 'Six Electric Concertos'. Not only is this album a pinnacle of rock chamber music, but it threw open the doors for a new kind of fusion-music, which in the '70s came to be called jazz-rock.

4

I was scratching my head and looking to the side when they took that picture.

7

Position that Claude Nobs uses when he's checking to find whether or not something is in quad.

10

A very obscure one, only used at one or two concerts. It's one of those 'finger in your ear' cues that you summon up if somebody said something funny in rehearsals and you want to relive or recapture it on stage. It's the optional cue, like, if I stick my finger in my ear right in the middle of a solo, that's to get ready. And then, I give the down-beat and then, we re-programme noise, or words, or physical actions after this.

5

Indicates play in 5/8 or 5/16 on cue.

8

You stop playing and you lean into the nearest microphone, and say "very interesting," spelled i-n-d-e-r-e-s-t-i-n-g, because that's the way Bruce Fowler says it.

6

The cue for a composite of noises that are sequenced out. If I lift up both sides of my hair, then play the whole sequence. If I lift up the right side of my hair, then play the first half of the sequence. If I lift up the second side of my hair, then play the second half. The sequence runs about twelve bars of just funny noise – they're having a laugh or another. It's called 'The Works.'

9

An indication that you are supposed to play a sharp, low grunt, like a low raised exclamation point in the middle of somebody's solo.

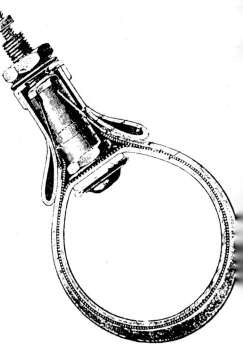

Jim Pons, F.Z, Ian Underwood, Mark Volman,Howard Kaylan, Don Preston, Aynsley Dunbar, 1970.

Castagnettes

1970 was a good year for Zappa in more ways than one. Despite the troubles of '69, The Mothers' split, he was as busy as ever. He continued work on 'Uncle Meat' (the film), and started another film project, *200 Motels*, as well as releasing 'Hot Rats'.

He also met two ex-members of The Turtles: Howard Kaylan and Mark Volman (rechristened Flo and Eddie), and Zubin Mehta. Together they gave a famous concert with the L.A. Philharmonic Orchestra on May 15 as part of a contemporary music festival.

Despite bad acoustics, which made proper recording impossible, it was a great success and earned many good reviews. Production work on *200 Motels* got off to a good start and Zappa continued his gruelling tour schedule, taking Flo and Eddie, George Duke, Ian Underwood and Aynsley Dunbar with him. 'Chunga's Revenge', a sort of warm-up to *200 Motels*, was also released, featuring Zappa on percussion and harpsichord.

Shooting for the film began in England in February 1971. A Royal Albert Hall concert was arranged, but was banned at the last moment by the managing body of the RAH who were horrified by some of the lyrics.

U.S. Tour, 1970

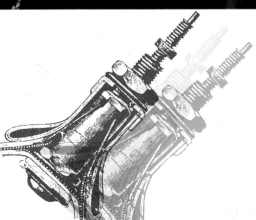

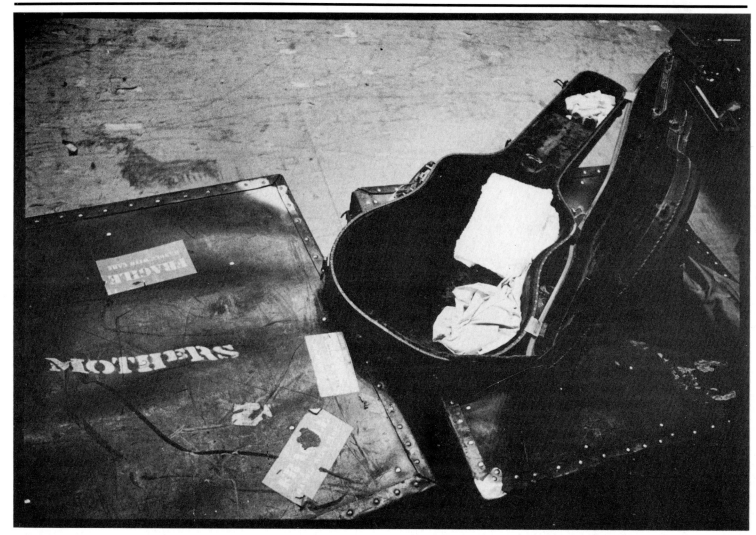

200 Motels is a full length production, filmed completely on video with a budget of $600,000, and then transferred on to 35mm. The cast included Theodore Bikel, Ringo Starr and Keith Moon. During rehearsals Jeff Simmons, the group's bassist, quit the band and walked out of the filming, finding it too much at odds with his personal image.

Zappa tried, and failed, to get Wilfred Bramble instead (who appeared in The Beatles' movie *Hard Day's Night* but is best known in the U.K. for his portrayal of Albert Steptoe in the comedy Steptoe and Son) then took on Ringo's chauffeur, Martin Lickert, once a bassist himself. Wary of Zappa's reputation, United Artists were suspicious of the film's contents and at first it was only shown in four cities, Los Angeles, Boston, Ann Arbor and Atlanta, before general release in January 1972.

As well as putting the finishing touches to the film during April and May '71, Zappa arranged two series of concerts. The first took place to mark the closure of Bill Graham's famous psychedelic ballroom, the Fillmore. John Lennon and Yoko Ono turned up on stage during these shows, much to the delight of the audience.

A double album was to be released with The Mothers/Lennon/Ono jam on one side, but Lennon's manager Allen Klein intervened. Eventually Zappa gave back the tape, refusing any financial deal. The jam resurfaced on Lennon's next album, but was poorly mixed and a purple passage concerning Flo, Eddie and Yoko was censored by Lennon and Phil Spector.

Lennon avenged Zappa's parody of the 'Sgt Pepper'sleeve by designing the inner sleeve of his 'Some Time In New York City' album as an imitation of The Mothers' live LP 'Fillmore East'.

Three months later Zappa came up with 'Billy The Mountain', a typically Zappa-esque mixture of absurdist 'Peter And The Wolf', 'Histoire du Soldat' (Stravinsky) and spy thriller pastiche. A shortened version can be found on 'Just Another Band From L.A.'.

This album marked the beginning of an unlucky period for Frank. The problems started on December 4 when fire broke out at the Casino de Montreux during a Mothers' concert, an incident immortalised by Deep Purple (some of whose members were in the audience) with 'Smoke on the Water'. As the equipment was destroyed, new instruments had to be bought for four concerts at London's Rainbow Theatre opening on December 10.

At the end of the first show, as Frank was taking his bows a certain Trevor Charles Howell climbed on stage and pushed Zappa down into the orchestra pit. Howell claimed he had not had his money's worth and also that his girlfriend had declared herself to be in love with Zappa. The object of these unwelcome attentions was picked up unconscious with a broken leg, his tour had to be cancelled, and the promotion of *200 Motels*, which was about to appear all over Europe, was in jeopardy. Howell was subsequently sentenced to nine months imprisonment.

The Grand Wazoo

There was one bright side to this unfortunate incident. Stuck in his wheelchair, Zappa composed like crazy, and before he was even fully recovered brought a band down to Paramount studios to record 'Waka/Jawaka' and 'The Grand Wazoo'.

This was no teeny-rock combo, but a very individual sort of big-band, bubbling with light touches of jazz and wah-wah guitar. The Grand Wazoo Orchestra (about twenty musicians, mostly recruited from the best L.A. studios) gave eight concerts in Europe and the U.S., but it was financially impractical), and towards the end of the year Zappa went off on tour again with the Little Wazoo (about eight musicians).

During the summer of 1972, in the midst of his Wazoo productions, Zappa also wrote 'Hunchentoot', a musical comedy. He organised the production and costumes and wrote a musical score, but it was never produced on Broadway as intended despite interest from Barbra Streisand's agents.

One of the striking things about Frank Zappa is that he has showed no inclination to be a studio musician although his skills as a producer, arranger, multi-instrumentalist and sound engineer would be ideal qualifications. On signing a new distribution deal with Warner Brothers he set up a new label, Discreet, which also signed Ted Nugent and Tim Buckley,* but most of all he wanted to get back on the road again. Success on stage bred success on record ('Overnite Sensation' had just come out), and Zappa's records sold more than ever.

'Apostrophe' followed 'Overnite...' high into the charts and Zappa was able to arrange a fitting celebration for his ten years of touring by hiring a brass band of 50 musicians to play in front of Warner Brothers Records offices. Things were going so well that he quickly released the live album 'Roxy And Elsewhere'. 'Roxy' is a fine monument to the concerts of this period, as was the next album, 'One Size Fits All'.

A TV show, 'A Token Of His Extreme', which was banned in the U.S. but appeared in Europe, also captures the magical sound of the band during this period.

*Tim Buckley was born on February 14, 1947, in Washington. He played in various country bands before being signed to Discreet by Herb Cohen. He died of a drug overdose on June 29, 1975.

Orchestral Favourites

Frank Zappa's career is full of strange twists and turns. He seemed happy with his wider popularity and his musicians, some of the best he had ever had, but he split the band and left manager Herb Cohen who he said had been taking rather too many liberties with the Discreet label.

He became reconciled with his old friend Don Vliet who suddenly stopped criticising Zappa in the press, and recounted earlier proclamations with statements like: "I'm sorry about what I said", "I didn't know what I was saying", and "Frank's a great guy". It didn't last and before long the irrepressible Captain was once again moaning about his former employer.

The result of their brief reconciliation was 'Bongo Fury' in 1975, the last album on Discreet. Zappa, who appeared to be moving in a funky-blues direction, rounded up 37 musicians to form the Abnuceals Emuukha Electric Orchestra. They recorded, and performed twice. Unfortunately a lack of co-operation by Warner Brothers led to these 'orchestral favourites' being released in an unworthily slapdash manner.

They eventually came out on record without the composer's consent, without final mixing, without credits for the musicians, and with two of the most ghastly sleeves in rock history, under the names 'Orchestral Favorites' and 'Studio Tan'.

From October 1975 to March 1976, Zappa was off on another world tour, and in May he broke off completely with Herb Cohen. While the inevitable lawsuit was in progress, Zappa was denied access to his own rehearsal room, and neither could he use his film and tape archives (which he only got back in 1982). He then recorded 'Zoot Allures', his last official album before 'Sheik Yerbouti'.

Christmas In New Jersey

Zappa, ever active, set out on another world tour in October 1976. In November he appeared on a number of television shows, notably Saturday Night Live, where he played the Purple Lagoon with the late John Belushi (of the Blues Brothers) in his celebrated portrayal of a samurai.

A series of Christmas shows between December 26 and 29 at the New York Palladium featured the Brecker Brothers, Ronnie Cuber, Tom Malone and many more. These concerts provided material for 'Live In New York' released in March 1977. But it was clear that relations between Zappa and Warner Bros were deteriorating. One of the songs for the album, 'Punky's Whips', speaks ironically about Terry Bozzio's passion for Punky Meadows, guitarist with the group Angel.

Terrified by the prospect of a libel suit with Meadows, Warners took it on themselves to withdraw the song, although Meadows himself said in a letter in Herb Cohen's possession that he liked it.

After this fiasco, things went from bad to worse between Zappa and Warners, and a lesser artist may well have been submerged by the subsequent avalanche of problems. Zappa sued Warners for breach of contract, refusal to pay for tapes already delivered, refusal to record new material during the specified period and unauthorised publication of his material. He also complained to the press about the treatment he received at the hands of his record company.

During his legal proceedings (which are now over – Zappa got both his tapes and his money back), he had to approach four different law firms before finding one with the guts to take on the powerful Warners empire. Meanwhile Zappa was also looking for a new record company. At first Capitol seemed interested but negotiations broke down, quite probably because Capitol had the same lawyers as Warners at the time, and also because Capitol pressed records for Warners.

Mercury/Polygram, however, had no such scruples and the first album was to be a four record set called 'Lather' (300 boxed sets exist), but just before the release date October 31, 1977, Warners informed Phonogram of their decision to release 'Live In New York', which was part of the set, and claimed that Phonogram had no right to release the 'Lather' set.

Barking Pumpkin

In late 1978, Zappa prepared 'Sheik Yerbouti', while working on the film *Baby Snakes*. In 1979 he was finally free to sign with Mercury for the U.S.A. and CBS for Europe. 'Sheik Yerbouti' was an immediate success and became his best seller to date. He had three law suits pending, but finally won back his 'old master' tapes from Verve and Warners.

Zappa continued to work as usual, combining long stints of world touring with an abundance of album releases. 'Baby Snakes' was a relative failure, though it won some awards, but his second rock opera 'Joe's Garage' was well received.

Relations were becoming strained between Zappa and CBS because Zappa was not prepared to make compromises, so he set up a new label of his own, Barking Pumpkin Records. Since then, free at last from any exclusive distribution set-up, Zappa has been floating from one crazy project to the next.

He brought out a three record set consisting entirely of guitar solos, made videos, published musical scores of his work, wrote articles in *Guitar Player*, had a photo novel published in 'Hustler', wrote the overall script/screenplay to his work ('Them Or Us', the book), made albums and still found time for one of his favourite pastimes, listening to classical orchestras play his music. This he did in Paris, with no less a man than Pierre Boulez, London and San Francisco.

There was also the three album musical comedy 'Thingfish' and the 'Old Masters' boxed set of the legendary early albums digitally remastered. He was almost hired to produce Bob Dylan's 'Infidels'.

Dylan turned up at Zappa's house, "in the freezing cold, with no coat and an open shirt. I sent someone down to check, to make sure it was not a Charles Manson, but it was him". He sat at the piano and played eleven songs and asked Zappa to produce his next album. Zappa recalled, "He doesn't have much of a sense of humour, but his new songs were nice, so I'd like to produce them though it would take a bit of adjustment. I said he should subcontract out the songs to Georgio Moroder to do a complete synthesiser track and Dylan should play guitar and harmonica over the top. It would be fantastic!"

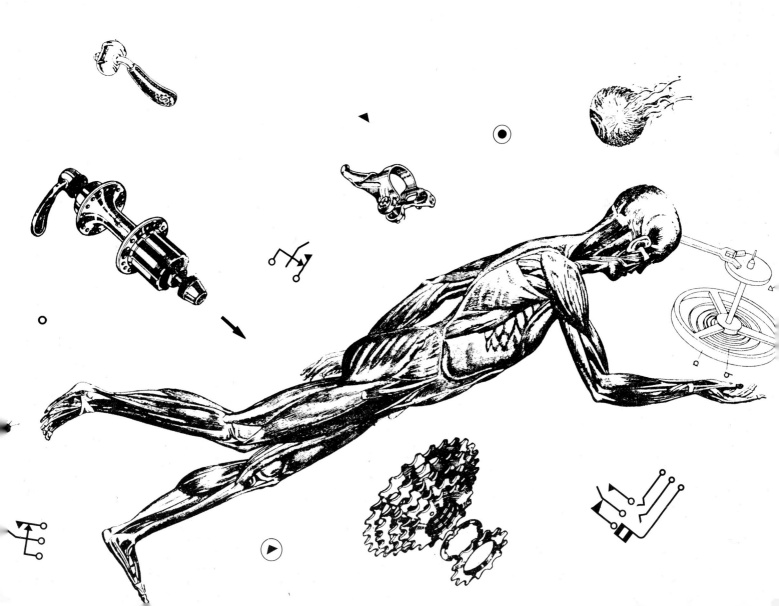

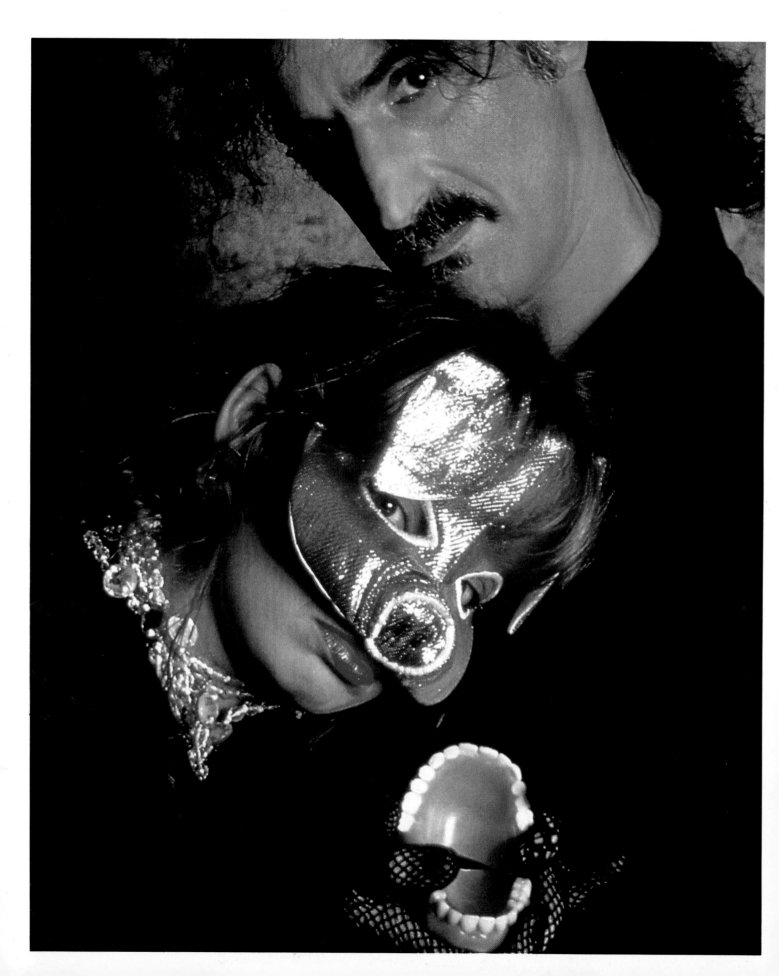

ZaPPA /iNSTRUCtiONS FOr Use

Friends

Zappa believes that no one in showbiz has any real friends: "It's very ruthless and it's very cold-hearted, and it has nothing to do with friendship. There's nothing more disgusting than people pretending to be friends while they're in business.

It's against the laws of nature because you know it's not sincere, so why should you have to put up with the added insult of this insincerity on top of the horribleness of the business?"

Love

"The way that people in America talk about love is totally incorrect. The American idea of love is ridiculous. It's a fantasy, a fairy-tale. It's based on goals that cannot be achieved and fantasies that just don't exist." (L.A. 1981.)

Money

"It's important in that without money I can't make records and can't do my art, because every piece of equipment I use costs money. Most of what I earn goes right back into the work which I do. The only thing that money means to me is whether or not I will have enough to do my next project.

If you're a poet, you don't need any equipment...but if you make records, you need a lot of other stuff, and nobody gives it to me." (L.A. 1981)

Approaching Nancarrow

Conlon Nancarrow was born in 1912 in the U.S.A., but has more recently lived in Mexico. For many years no-one paid much attention to this bright old man who will be considered one of the most important composers of the late twentieth century, and who has already been praised by Boulez, Ligeti, Cage and Zappa, although he nearly got brushed under the carpet of history.

It was a strange turn of events, helped by support from Charles Amirkhanian and

Cage, as well as Zappa's frequent references to him in interviews in relation to 'Uncle Meat' or 'Envelopes'. He also mentions him on stage ('Peaches III'). Nancarrow was also present at the Pierre Boulez IRCAM concert.

What is so interesting about Nancarrow's 'Studies For Mechanical Piano'? Firstly, it is an exhaustive investigation of new possibilities in rhythm, tempo, musical texture and polyphony.

On the one hand, there is enough going on in these pieces to satisfy even the most abstract Constructivist, while on the other, there is enough freedom and lyricism to warm the heart of the most romantic listener.

At some moments the music is hard, austere, cold as ice, at others it has a hot, explosive exuberance. Zappa says: "Some of it sounds like ragtime, that's totally bionic!". Now that he has decided to compose more with his Barking Pumpkin Digital Gratification Consort, a computer and synclavier, it looks as if Nancarrow's work will come to acquire an importance for Zappa similar to that of Varèse's.

Captain Beefheart
Don Van Vliet

Don Van Vliet was born in Glendale in 1941. When very small, he was interested in sculpting little objects representing animals. He was so involved in his sculptures that his parents sometimes had to slide his meals under the bedroom door.

He finally attracted professional attention and met the sculptor Augustonia Rodriguez while visiting Griffith Park Zoo.

His career as a musician began in Lancaster, at the edge of the desert in southern California, where he met Zappa at high-school. At the time, he was listening to blues from the Mississippi Delta as well as avant-garde jazz musicians like Ornette Coleman and Cecil Taylor. He briefly played in a band called The Omens with Alex St. Claire and Zappa in 1963, but his main interest was still sculpture, and he enrolled for a course at Antelope Valley Junior College.

However, he quickly became suspicious of what was written in the text-books, and went to work as manager of a chain of shoe shops before going to Cucamonga where he teamed up again with Zappa, who was composing and arranging film music at the time. He and Zappa decided to make a film, *Captain Beefheart Meets The Grunt People*, but the project was finally abandoned in about 1968. Zappa left for Los Angeles and Don Vliet returned to Lancaster where he formed 'The Desert Musicians' with some friends.

There was record company interest, and his first single was a cover version of Bo Diddley's 'Diddy Wah Diddy'. But Jerry Moss at A&M was scared by other songs and refused to release an LP. Beefheart had to wait until 1965 when Bob Krasnow at Kama Sutra Records agreed to release the same material under the name 'Safe As Milk'. The Beefheart legend was underway, and there are many stories about his astonishing vocal register breaking microphones.

His guitarist quit the band just before Monterey Pop Festival which was a catastrophe as Beefheart's music was such

that he needed several months to shape a new musician to his highly individual style.

Beefheart signed to Buddah and once he had left Kama Sutra, Krasnow released 'Strictly Personal'. New relationships sprang up which were characterised by a mixture of love and hate between the Captain and those with whom he worked. He fell out with Krasnow, and later with Zappa, although Frank gave him his first opportunity to record an album unconditionally. This was the famous 'Trout Mask Replica', one of the most extreme albums in rock history.

For the first time ever, Beefheart was satisfied with the result, but not for long. He was not happy with being put in the same bracket as Alice Cooper or the GTO's by the people at Bizarre/Straight, although he returned to contribute vocals on Zappa's 'Willie The Pimp' ('Hot Rats').

In 1975, after making amends for insulting Zappa in the American press, the pair of them toured together and recorded 'Bongo Fury'. But they soon fell out again, and now Beefheart lives a reclusive life, withdrawn from the world at the edge of the Mojave desert among rare animals and plants.

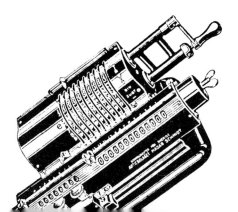

Discipline

"There's no substitute for discipline, and it's the first thing a musician must learn when they join the band. I don't mean punishment, but respect for the fact that we work collectively, as a group. Musicians are some of the laziest people on earth, and think that the rest of the world will shower them with benefits because they're so good, but they're wrong. If you want to make a record or tour, you have to start by working as hard as you can, practising, expanding on your limitations. If you can't do that yourself, you need someone to push you, and that's all I do. I ask musicians to do things they've never had the opportunity to do before. Afterwards when they leave, they say 'free at last!' and then they do nothing more because there's no one there to encourage them to open out. Most of them have stopped progressing after leaving the band."
(*From* Rock & Folk *No.161*).

Drugs

Zappa has often spoken out against drugs. "I am talking about anything that alters your perception to the point where you think you're something other than what you really are, and you start behaving accordingly, and in L.A. at the height of the drug frenzy, we had people who thought they could fly. LSD had convinced them of this.

"Well, if you want to be clinical about it, you can take each of the drugs, you can analyse what they do to your body, and you can analyse what they have done to the different parts of the society that have used them, and depending on what your values are, and how much you appreciate the performance of a person in a society who is not drug-altered, you'll be doing these things in different ways. In other words, I think LSD was bad, because it confused a lot of people and probably caused brain damage.

"I mean, there are people that I knew that I see now, who used a lot of LSD, who are just wasted. They can hardly tie their own shoes you know, they are gone. Then,

you have people who smoke an awful lot of marijuana, because it's really, really groovy and just for relaxing, and their memories are fucked. They can't remember things. One musician I know lost his sense of rhythm you know, and they lost equilibrium, but they are very groovy, and they are very laid-back and mellow and having a wonderful time. But something was taken out of them, you know, that should have been there in order to make them function better in society.

"I don't like alcohol, I don't like chit-chat, I don't like social intercourse. I don't like being put in a position where I have to deal with other people's emotional freight. When a person takes drugs or uses alcohol, they think they are giving themselves a license to be an asshole, because they can always say, 'Whoops! I'm sorry, I was so stoned I didn't know what I was doing', and suddenly that makes everything OK. All I require if somebody is on my payroll is that they don't use drugs and don't have any drugs in their possession at the time they are performing a service for me. What they do in their spare time with their private lives is their business, but once they are on the road, they are representing me, and I'm footing the bill for their total lifestyle. I'm providing their hotel, their food and transportation. I am paying their salary. I'm doing all these things and in exchange they are supposed to make themselves available and competent to play concerts for the audience that comes to the places expecting a show. Now, if they get ripped and can't play they are letting the audience down, and they are doing it in such a way that the blame goes on me."
(*Headley Gritter.*)

28

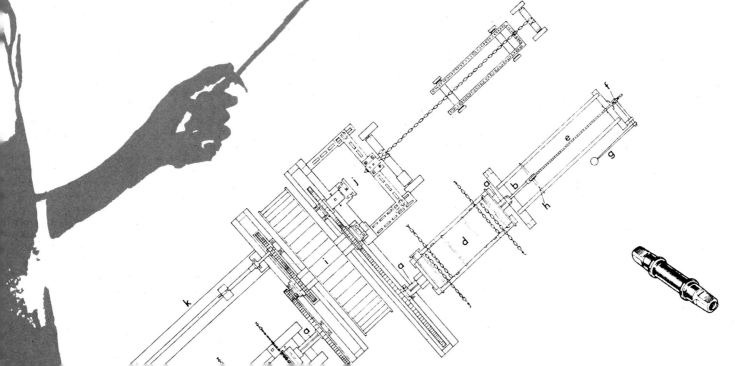

Guitars

Frank Zappa began playing guitar at eighteen. He knew nothing about chords, so he bought Mickey Baker's guitar tutorial. At this time, he was mostly listening to things like 'Three Hours Past Midnight', by Johnny 'Guitar' Watson, or 'Story Of My Life' by Guitar Slim.

Although he was disinclined to imitate their style, he was influenced by their melodic approach. His first electric guitar was a rented Fender Telecaster, followed by a Jazzmaster. With the money he earned from the film *Run Home Slow*, he bought the Gibson ES-5 Switchmaster, which can be heard on his first three albums.

Later Zappa used a Les Paul Gold and a Gibson SG. Today he has all manner of guitars, including one that belonged to Jimi Hendrix which was burnt at a Miami rock festival and which can be heard on 'Zoot Allures'. Zappa was one of the first players to use a wah-wah pedal, and you can hear it on clarinet, saxophone and guitar in 'We're Only In It For The Money', 1967.

This was around the time that Hendrix was playing at the Café-A-Go-Go, right next to the Garrick Theater where The Mothers were performing their show 'Pigs And Repugnants'.

Zappa prefers playing guitar live because in the studio he must keep his eye on other matters. Much of his best guitar work has been accomplished live, especially as he doesn't compose a solo before playing it.

He often uses a set base of about twenty bars; so strictly speaking it is neither a composition nor a complete improvisation, but a collage-like mixture of the two. His solos are influenced by the rhythm of words, and melody is one of his greatest interests.

When a new musician joins the band, Frank explains his ideas on rhythm, which is often based on a cyclical sequence of calm, sustained periods, and surges of quadruple quavers. Zappa denies that he is a guitar hero, but sees himself as a composer who plays the guitar. He also rejects the show-biz myth that to be good, you have to be the fastest, the 'prettiest', or the loudest.

Zappa has clear-cut ideas about the guitar. According to him, the confusion started when English bands started weaning Americans on to recycled 1950's music played by people who were much younger and prettier than the original bluesmen. "How many Stones fans have heard of Slim Harpo or Muddy Waters?" he asks. Zappa thinks that the best guitar in the 1960's came from Jeff Beck, with his use of feedback, and from Jimi Hendrix's revolutionary sounds. That is the good side, but there is also a bad one: 'twanging' twelve-string folk rock. With regard to later developments, he is even more virulent. "Let's be frank", he says, "Once you've learnt the most common 28 or 29 rock chords, a few country licks here, a bit of Albert King there, you go and steal some silly clothes off your grandmother. You'll get a contract and sell ten million copies.

"Then another young guitarist hears you jerking around at phenomenal speed with your fuzz... you'll become part of '70s guitar history...just be patient, your time will come. In a world such as this, who needs to know the original sources?"

For Frank Zappa, nothing sounds quite like a good old guitar with its distortion, and although you can analyse this and break down its harmonics, there's always something extra. An old guitar of distinguished pedigree has an emotional content that goes beyond that of other instruments, and nothing sounds as blasphemous as a guitar whose capacity for distortion is used properly.

Zappa was one of the first to use fuzz which Paul Buff, who sold him the studio in 1964, also experimented with. In 1962 Zappa and Captain Beefheart recorded a manic version of 'Slippin' And Slidin'' (Little Richard), but when Zappa took the tape to Dot Records, they said: "We can't release this racket! It's noise, that's all."

Garni Du Jour

Zappa understands a simple philosophy: "Americans hate music, but they love entertainment. The reason they hate music is that they've never stopped to listen to what musical content is, because they're so befuddled by the packaging and merchandising surrounding the musical material they've been induced to buy.

There's so much peripheral stuff that helps them make their analysis of what music is...It's the Garni du Jour syndrome: You go buy a hamburger. If somebody gives you a hamburger on a dish it means one thing. If somebody gives you a hamburger on a dish with a piece of green stuff and a wrinkled carrot and a radish, it's a Deluxe Hamburger. It's still the same piece of dog meat on the inside, but it's got a Garni du Jour...In music too, the way in which material is presented is equally important as what's on the record."

Grandmothers

The Grandmothers, led by Don Preston and the brothers Gardner, are not on good terms with their ex-boss, and this seems to annoy Zappa: "No doubt it's the coolest thing they could find to do. If they want to get a wider public they might find it easier by calling me an asshole. But is there any artistic defense for what they do? They've never paid me for my compositions they play, they use my name to promote themselves and they're not even grateful. If you knew what they were like when they were in the band compared to what they're doing now, you'd say 'It's a fake!'. They literally massacre the pieces."

Jazz

Zappa has always claimed he is unenthusiastic about jazz: "There's no passion in it. It's a bunch of people trying to be cool, looking for the certification of an intellectual community. Most of today's jazz is even more worthless than the most blatantly commercial music because it pretends to be something it's not. I'd rather stay away from that".

Despite these words, on closer inspection it appears that Zappa has frequently worked with jazz musicians both in and out of the studio. This is probably because the essential quality he wants from his musicians is 'flexibility'.

As well as his great interest in Dolphy, Mingus and Wes Montgomery, Zappa took on Buzz Gardner, who had played with André Hodeir at St. Germain-des-Prés (Paris) in the '50s and Gene Di Novi who was with Buddy Rich, Benny Goodman and Anita O'Day. The list is long: Don Preston, (Carla Bley, Don Ellis, Gil Evans), Chad Wackerman (Bill Watrous), Mike Lang (Don Ellis), Pete Jolly (Shorty Rogers, Buddy Di Franco), John Guerin (Jimmy Smith), Frankie Capp (Stan Kenton), Shelly Manne, Victor Feldman, Dennis Budimir, Emil Richards.

There are also more famous ones, like Jean Luc Ponty, and Sugarcane Harris. Recently, there have been specialists in fusion music like Tom Malone, the Brecker Brothers, Fowler, David Samuels, Ronnie Cuber, Wilton Felder, as well as the disconcerting Buell Neidlinger and George Duke. Roland Kirk, who played with The Mothers at Boston, later wrote: "It was great. People are wrong to criticize popular musicians playing jazz, especially when they have Zappa's class. Purists may close their ears and look disdainful, and a lot of people think they're a genius if nobody comes to listen to them, but they will often find that the pop 'morons' have gone a lot further than they have…"

Johnny Guitar Watson

Johnny 'Guitar' Watson was born in Houston on February 3, 1935. His father taught him piano and he became interested in guitar at eleven after hearing Clarence 'Gatemouth' Brown and T-Bone Walker.

At 15 Johnny was in L.A. having just finished his studies, and he attracted sufficient attention to be recruited by Johnny Otis. He also worked with people like Chuck Higgins and Amos Milburn. His various jobs established his reputation and with 'Space Guitar' he showed that he was a long way ahead of his time in his use of feedback and reverb. Johnny 'Guitar' Watson, (he took his nickname after seeing the film 'Johnny Guitar') has been called 'The Gangster Of Love' and 'The Original Rapper'. His prolific style explodes in shouts, slides, murmurs and moans of both guitar and voice.

Zappa discovered him while still an adolescent in the 1950s, and Watson is among the biggest influences on his guitar style, along with Guitar Slim. Today he's probably the only musician extant for whom Zappa has serious respect. Zappa even thought of having Watson in his band after 'One Size Fits All' along with Chester Thompson, Ruth Underwood and George Duke. Zappa was not alone in admiring Johnny 'Guitar' Watson.

In interviews, Jimi Hendrix often stated humbly that Watson taught him everything. "I was interested in his electric guitar experiments, and when he played it with his teeth, behind his back or on his head". Praise indeed from Hendrix, who is celebrated for similar stylistic accomplishments.

Zappa says: "When I was at high school, I used to listen to Watson's blues records. They made me crazy! For a year, I went to eat at the same restaurant serving chilli,

because they had 'Three Hours Past Midnight' on the juke box. I listened to it three times over lunch.

I also had another copy at home to play in the evenings."

Music

Zappa believes that music is an art form too, good for our society, that music is too subtle and beautiful to be appreciated by the average American.

Musicians

"Each time I get a new musician, I have to mould the new replacement. This takes time and money, and it would be easier and cheaper for me to keep the same band, but I don't want to keep anybody who isn't totally dedicated to the work. If their mind is elsewhere, I don't want them. There are too many excellent musicians who dream of taking their place. I get cassettes, letters, musical scores, from all over the world because I have the only group which is important, well-known and long-lasting, which anybody can join if they're good enough. I audition everybody who comes up, and I'm the only one who offers this opportunity. There's no way you could join a band like Led Zeppelin, but musicians know that my door is never closed."
(From Rock & Folk *No.161, F. Vincent & J.M. Bailleux.)*

Boss

"I write the music. I pay the bills. I hire people to make the music. What I've written down on paper, somebody must play. I don't play all instruments. I provide money for people to run their lives because they play notes that I write. Other than that, I don't need to comment. I don't need to have committee meetings to do it. It's a very simple relationship. But guess who my boss is? My boss is the audience. They rely on me to hire the best musicians that I can find and to train them as well as I can in order to bring that music to an audience in the best condition possible for the money that they pay for the ticket. I'm directly employed by the audience".

Politics

Zappa reckons America is heading for a new phase of McCarthyism: "The conservative movement in the U.S. is trying to control peoples' ideas as it hasn't done for many years. It's not a question of people on the right being financially cautious, but what Reagan's re-election brought was a number of people like those idiots at the Supreme Court who really are on the right of Attila The Hun. It's the new Dark Ages of Them Or Us."

Zappa also believes that the boom in video 'religion' in politics is indicative of this. For 'You Are What You Is', Zappa made a video which showed a man who looked like Reagan being strapped to an electric chair. The video was refused by virtually all TV networks.

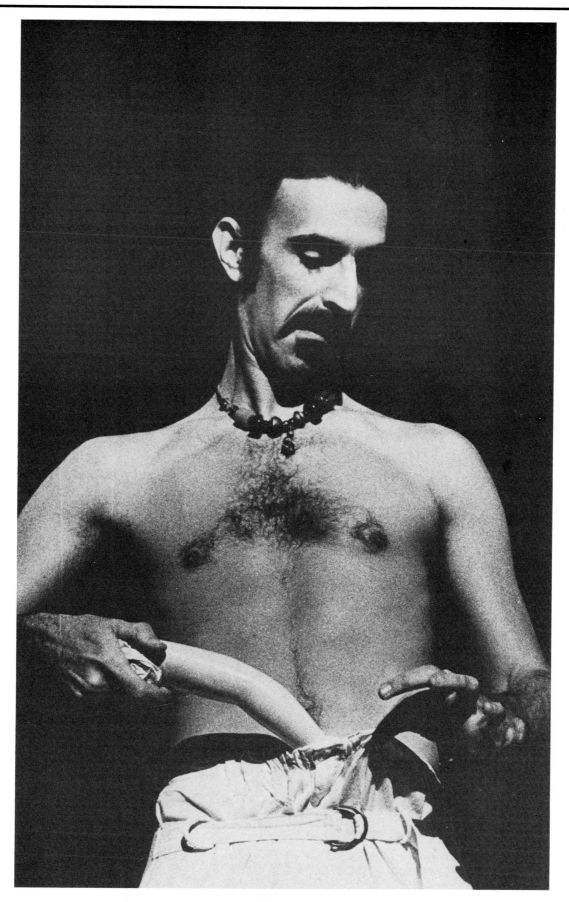

Recruitment

Zappa has discovered a number of musicians who went on to become famous in their own right, including Beefheart, Adrian Belew, George Duke, Terry Bozzio and Tim Buckley. They were lucky enough to be recruited by him, and their creativity was subsequently stimulated by the Zappa environment.

"First of all", says Zappa, "I go out on the street, and most rock and roll people who have a name don't do that. I don't go to bars just looking for musicians, but I know what I like, and I can spot a talent, like in Nashville where I found Adrian Belew. I'll take the guys from someone else. When they come into my group they have the chance to work with better equipment, they get some discipline, they get a chance to be seen by hundreds of thousands of people, they get mentioned in interviews and stuff. Hey presto…they're fantastic musicians!"

Musicians join Zappa's band for a number of reasons and during their time in it are assured of a certain level of comfort, but if they think they can do better elsewhere, Zappa does not try to keep them.

Some of them become famous, others don't. Working with Zappa is strenuous but it's no labour camp. To get into the band you have to be good, and if you want to leave, the door is always open because there's always someone just as well qualified waiting outside to take your place.

Part of Zappa's job is recruiting people and judging their capabilities as accurately as possible, so ensuring that the quality of the performance does not deteriorate. Flexibility is a must, as Zappa likes writing in different styles, and no one group is perfect for each style.

Sex

Asked whether his views on sex are unorthodox, Zappa replies: "What's so funny about songs to do with sex? Sure, if you say 'Fuck me, suck me' it's considered to be American art, but people don't like it when I remind them that the sexual terms they expect are so useless. They hate it and throw their frustrations back on me, but I'm just a reporter.

"I've dealt with sex ever since I've been writing songs and can see no reason not to do so. Pretending that sex doesn't exist is plain idiotic."

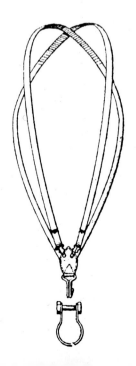

Shut Up And Play Yer Guitar

Zappa released this album at the express demand of fans who wanted to hear more of his onstage guitar work. Another album of a similar kind is in the pipeline, and this kind of instrumental music has sold very well.

Studio

Zappa generally discusses electrical effects with his sound engineers before using them, as there is always a difference between what you hear on tape and a finished album, but when it comes to musical detail, he makes the decisions. If somebody else thinks he has a better idea, he is politely asked to keep quiet and do what he has been shown. Zappa says, "It is impossible to ask people's opinion every time you press a button. It's long enough as it is with all the overdubbing."

Synthesizers

For a composer like Zappa, "The first thing you have to do is learn how to speak to the synthesizer player. You have to know all the basic language concerning what the instrument is dealing with. You have to know what an oscillator is, you have to know what a filter is…so when you tell the guy, 'No that's wrong' I want more of *this*,' you're not telling him in romantic terms, you're saying, 'Give me more frequency modulation.'" To do this, Zappa bought an ARP 2600, read the manual and taught himself. Then, he got a mini-moog and others, and worked on getting to grips with their different characteristics. He also uses Syndrums and guitar synths. On stage his electronic instruments offer a wide range of music variations: as well as an EMU that often stays at home, the band has a Rhodes, an Electrocamp, a mini-moog, a clavinet and an ARP 2600 played by one of the keyboardists. The other can use a Yamaha Electric Grand, an ARP String, a Hammond, another clavinet, or a Roland.

Recording Techniques

Zappa's equipment is especially good for sound editing. The tapes can be cut and rearranged on to the master tape in a variety of ways, often numerically according to the rhythms, which can create a collage effect with different sound textures. Most of his recordings are taken from live performances to which re-recordings are added. To combat bad acoustics in the auditoria he plays, Zappa uses an MSL 3 system, linked to his mobile studio, (100 inputs, 3 video circuits, 3 consoles, Neve/Midas/Carvin). As regards microphones, Zappa uses AKG, PZM and Neuman U 87, as well as some older ones. He also has some almost 'antique' effects like the Poultec, the Kepex and the Scamps. Zappa considers working at the console comparable to that of a modern conductor, bringing out the qualities and contrasts of the different instruments. To improve the quality of his recordings, he has also bought an excellent Sony PCM digital.

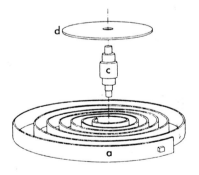

Video

"People who think of videos as an art form are probably the same people who think Cabbage Patch Dolls are a revolutionary form of soft sculpture. The whole intention of doing a video is to sell a record. Most artists who make videos are just dummies who stand in front of the camera, along with the rented cute girl who mouths the words occasionally. They're starting to look the same, mainly because there are a handful of top-flight guys who charge exorbitant prices. These people, the ones who are being used to do the slick videos, are the same people who do the beer commercials. I mean…it's just commercials. When you watch something, more than fifty percent of what you experience is visual so the music is always subordinate to the visual. So ultimately, making a video is to do something which is anti-music. It forces your song, such as it is, into a secondary position while people pay attention to what the images are, and the images aren't yours. Then, to add insult to injury, you pay. The company doesn't pay, you pay".

Zappa believes that reports on how videos influence record sales are exaggerated, and thinks that the radio is more important because, "You can watch a video maybe six times before you want to puke over it, but you can listen to a record hundreds of times if you like it."

Pattern Recognition And Storage Capacity (Or Speed).

"The main thing a person has to have is very fast pattern recognition and information storage capacity. That's because we play a two to two and a half hour show non stop with everything organized. There are solos, and these are improvised, but the sequence of events is planned out so that the audience doesn't have to sit around and wait for something to happen."

Zappa often gets his musicians to learn about 70 pieces, some of which are very complex and played without musical score. This demands an ability to memorise rapidly because, "You can't spend a year, teaching somebody a show." For the last few years, Zappa has rehearsed for up to two months before going on tour, five days a week, six to ten hours a day, with complete equipment and a rehearsal budget of $13,250 weekly. Musicians have to know or learn how to handle polyrhythms, have good stage presence, and be able to play their instrument in a variety of styles from R&B to modernist compositions. He has often been surprised to find that many musicians who have mastered one particular style are virtually ignorant of other styles.

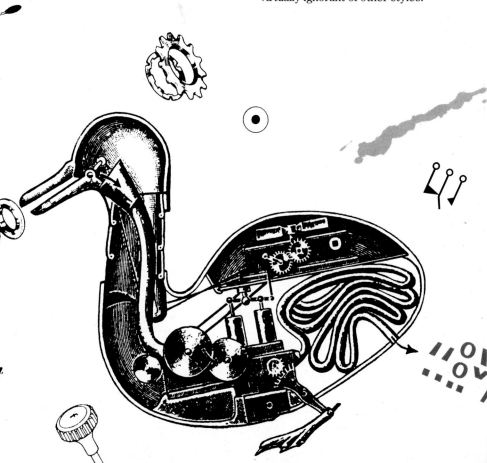

3

tHE ZaPPA MeNAgErie

The Mothers Of Destruction. Paris 1968.

Frank Zappa is certainly a law unto himself, but although his multiple talents as guitarist, conductor, arranger and more put him firmly in control of the creative wheels, he still needs others to help him keep them turning, and a wide variety of characters have travelled on these wheels. He has dealt with such a diverse and even conflicting group of people that it is necessary to further give him credit as both a catalyst and talent spotter. In fact, Zappa is the ringleader of a modern musical theatre, and has been driving his ever changing menagerie in and out of various continents for the last twenty years.

What is the connection between old friend Ray Collins, an ex- carpenter, and Lowell George, who cropped up on *'Weasels Ripped My Flesh'* before going on to found Little Feat with, among others, Roy Estrada? Roy is another of the old faithfuls, a mild mannered guy who worked alongside Zappa from 1964 until the dissolution of the original Mothers Of Invention, and later rejoined Uncle Frank on the '76 Japanese tour, *'Baby Snakes'*, *'The Man From Utopia'* and *'Them Or Us'* after a spell in a mental institution. He also teamed up with Beefheart as part of the Magic Band with Art Tripp and Elliot Ingber. They adopted the names Orejon (Estrada), Ed Marimba (Art Tripp) and Winged Eel Fingerling (Ingber).

Ian, Ruth, Don And A Few Others...

Art Tripp, a model student with a diploma in percussion and an ex-member of the Cincinnati Symphonia, certainly had his mind stretched while with The Mothers. He became so perturbed by his extreme experiences with Zappa and Beefheart that he gave up music altogether for a while to become an insurance salesman, only to resurface later on a Donna Summer tour.

Ian Underwood

Don Preston

Thompson hires his services out to Genesis, Phil Collins and Santana. There is no news of Ruth, but Ian is now in a studio programming synthesizers for funky L.A. starlets. Amen.

The first generation Mothers also included Jimmy Carl Black, the 'Indian of the group', and the man behind Geronimo Black, the first anti-Zappa band. With the money he earned with The Mothers, Jimmy wanted to open a sweetshop to feed his numerous children but this did not last, and he returned as a country and western singer (hard for an Indian!) on '200 Motels' and 'You Are What You Is'. He stooped to following the unrepentant moanings of Don Preston and Bunk and Buzz Gardner before becoming reconciled with Frank. Don Preston, the mad scientist, and electronic manipulator, has a healthily manic style that corresponds to the wilder side of Zappa's music, contrasting with the colder technical ability of the Gardner brothers. Don has played gigs with Meredith Monk and Carla Bley, and Bunk and Buzz appeared with André Hodeir at St. Germain-des-Prés, Paris, in the 1950s.

The Mothers also had their prototype John Belushi (of the film *1941*) in the shape of

ambition, who is probably the only person on earth that Zappa actually hates. Zappa did much to boost Ponty to fame, and must have noted with interest that this French violinist even managed to cross swords with the sweet-tempered John Maclaughlin.

After their time with The Mothers, ex-Turtles Flo and Eddie (Mark Volman and Howard Kaylan) never really managed to find their niche, which must be somewhere between Cheech and Chong and The Blues Brothers, but they are still jogging along in their own special way.

Ian Underwood, another important figure, met Zappa after seeing the Garrick Theatre shows, and turned up again at Apostolic Studios where Zappa was recording. Ian explained that he was a Bachelor of Music from Yale, holder of a Master's Degree in Composition from Berklee, a trained pianist specializing in Mozart, and could play saxophone. No doubt he was too modest to add that he could also play the organ and clarinet, and could read even the toughest musical scores. This was in August 1967 and was hardly commonplace in a rock band then, or any other time. Zappa showed him the instruments and said. "OK, whip it out!". Of course, Ian was taken on, and he tells the story on '*Uncle Meat*'.

Ian also brought along his girlfriend, Ruth Komanoff, who had just completed percussion course. She later became Mrs Underwood and contributed a splendid velocity to albums such as '*Overnite Sensation*'. The Underwoods exerted a big influence on Zappa by freeing him from having to limit the complexity of his musical scores. Ian, virtually a one man band, became one of Zappa's privileged accomplices and even wrote piano arrangements for him ('*Little House*'). A little later Ruth became the virtuoso – and irreplaceable – percussionist of '*One Size Fits All*'. With George Duke and Chester Thompson, she helped make up what many consider to be the best incarnation of The Mothers. Today, George Duke is pursuing a successful solo career, while Chester

Ruth Underwood

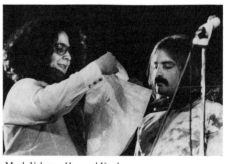

Mark Volman, Howard Kaylan

Jim 'Motorhead' Sherwood and his incredible pilot's helmet. Before playing saxophone and tambourine, Jim was a car-repair man who used to fix the motor that Zappa and the Captain once drove. He has now returned to the country, with his pilot's helmet of course.

There is no sense in wasting words over Jean Luc Ponty, the little man with the big

Looking back, it can be seen that few of the original Mothers were destined to emerge from Zappa's inventions afloat, although with the second generation matters are different. They were technically better musicians and have nearly always found musical work (Underwood, Thompson) and even solo success (Duke). The new 'youngsters' (this is an accurate description: in 1981 the average age of the band was twenty-one, and some of them were taken on at nineteen) grapple with the music in a fine display of willingness. For them Zappa's music is a sort of ladder-cum-research lab. This will doubtless lead to a degree from the Zappa School Of Music, where discipline worthy of a Samurai meets Zen self-transcendence. (Zappa himself got interested in Zen in the early '60s). They now have a prestigious calling-card.

Warren Cucurullo

Warren Cucurullo hails from Brooklyn, and when he was just an adolescent he completely 'flashed out' on Zappa. It was the start of a great adventure. He taught himself *all* Zappa's songs at home and not only that, for years he learned all of his hero's guitar solos note for note! Wherever he went he took a bag full of Zappa cassettes. Several years passed until one day the two of them met. Zappa was impressed by this fan who knew so much about him, and took Warren to meet the other musicians. His dream was soon to come true...he played with The Mothers. Warren's arrival stirred up the group's internal chemistry and stimulated professionals such as Tommy Mars and Peter Wolf. He seemed at ease in the Zappa universe and the others appreciated this. Zappa himself liked this young guy whose combination of precocious talent, amateur background and devotion to the Boss made him strongly reminiscent of the first generation Mothers.

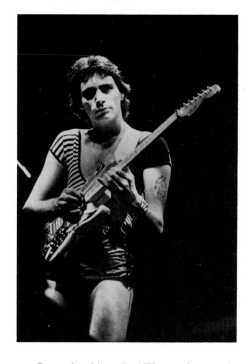

Soon after his arrival Warren frequently took on the role of a sort of onstage Zappa understudy when Frank wanted to concentrate on other areas. This included contributing both to guitar work and to the clownish element within the band. Sometimes he took over the parody aspect of The Mothers, which enabled Frank to indulge in some of his favorite pleasures, like conducting the band, or listening to the music as a spectator over a coffee and cigarette, without being constantly distracted by his own inventions. Zappa thus became the first listener/spectator to his own music. This explains his famous self-distancing from the group on stage, which some have mistakenly assumed to be boredom.

Between gigs Warren was often asked to sit with Frank in the dressing room or on the bus and practise new solos. He left the band (on good terms with Zappa) to form Missing Persons with Patrick O'Hearn and Terry Bozzio, and was replaced by Steve Vai.

Steve Vai. 'The Little Italian Virtuoso'

Steve Vai began playing musical instruments very young. At fourteen, he gave up the accordion to play guitar, took a course on music theory and went to the Boston School of Music, Berklee. Steve is a great fan of Zappa's music and at seventeen, bored with Berklee, he transcribed 'Black Page' and sent it to Zappa, along with a cassette of his band Morning Thunder. Frank replied that he would take him on immediately, not as a guitarist, but as a transcriber. During his eighteenth and nineteenth years Steve transcribed *all* of Zappa's guitar solos (see the Guitar Book) which he finished just in time to go on the 1982 tour. His no holds barred guitar style, somewhere between Hendrix and Van Halen, was a great success, and while Zappa made contact with the audience, Steve kept the often difficult guitar work going. it was almost a personal challenge.

Steve responds furiously to those who say Zappa exploits his musicians by making them play parts he could not do himself. "People say that Zappa can't play everything he writes, but how many composers whose main instrument is the piano have also written parts for violin? Maybe he can't play all the instruments, but he knows exactly how his pieces should sound, and whether or not it's correct. For it to sound right, all you have to do is play the correct notes with the appropriate feeling and emotion. The musicians Frank has had recently, myself included, work at the pieces we find difficult until we can play them. It's a question of pride. Frank never asks something of you that he knows you can't do. When he gives you a piece of written music, he asks 'Can you play this?'. You think to yourself, 'I'll be a better musican if I manage it', and the thought of how bad it would be not to be able to play something he's given you, fills you with the energy necessary to learn it. You find that you can play things you never thought you were capable of."

Adrian Belew. The Guitar Rhinoceros

Zappa discovered Adrian Belew at a club in Nashville, and made a note of his phone number. A few months later he called and asked him to an audition. This did not go too well, and Adrian, frustrated and afraid he would be turned down, took Zappa to one side and said, "Frank, I'm not used to having all these roadies and people around me. Let's go somewhere quiet and I'll show you what I can really do". He was hired. When Zappa called him he could not read music, but he soon learnt.

One day, during rehearsals, Zappa told him that as there was no part for him to play in one of the pieces, he should dress up as a female soldier and parade around the stage waggling his behind. Adrian was a success at this, and can be seen performing this sketch in the film 'Baby Snakes'. Another time, Zappa showed him a song, part of which

seemed so Dylan-ish that Adrian could not resist singing it as such. The excellent result, plus harmonica, is *'Flakes', ('Sheik Yerbouti')*.

Adrian says, "I was educated into a lot of music after I got in the band. When I'd be staying at Frank's house he'd say, 'Listen to this, listen to that.' Once, he said 'I'm going to turn you on to this guy Edgar Varèse, who's my hero in so many ways. This is who I listen to'. So I was intently listening to this bizarre, powerful music, really enjoying it, and the dogs outside started barking. I said, 'Wow, you know those dogs fit right in with the music', and he said, 'Adrian, you're beautiful'". Soon Adrian's talents were interesting others. Brian Eno told David

Adrian Belew

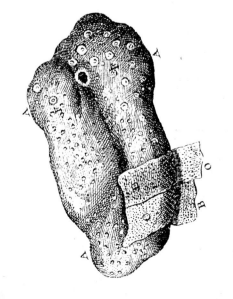

Bowie about Belew's musicianship, and when Zappa played Berlin, Bowie was backstage. At the end of the tour he was hired for Bowie's *'Lodger'* album, and the rest of his career is common knowledge: Bowie, Sakamoto, Talking Heads, King Crimson, Tom Tom Club, and more.

Zappa As Producer

Zappa is a talented record producer who has attracted various production offers from established artists, notably Kraftwerk *('The Man Machine')* and Dylan *('Infidels')*, although neither of these came to fruition. His production career got off to a rather low key start with two tracks for The Animals on *'Animalisms'*. Next came a double album of Lenny Bruce's poetry *('Berkeley Concert')* on his own label, followed by an aural documentary on busking street singer Wildman Fischer. Then came two productions which are unquestionably masterpieces: Beefheart's *'Trout Mask Replica'* and the GTO's album, which narrates the sexual adventures of these famous groupies and features such illustrious musicians as Nicky Hopkins, Jeff Beck and Rod Stewart.

Miss Christine, one of the GTOs, was governess to Zappa's children. She appears on the *'Hot Rats'* cover, and had a close relationship with a certain Vincent Furnier, who later changed his name to Alice Cooper. Much critical ink has been spilled over Alice Cooper, but Zappa maintains that his decadent image and bizarre clothes, which influenced such diverse musicians as The New York Dolls, Gary Glitter, Bowie and Roxy Music, were originally invented by Miss Christine alone. She tragically destroyed herself, although it is said she was vital in helping her ex-lover's rise to fame. Rejected by Vincent Furnier, who owed her so much, she died of a heroin overdose on November 5, 1972.

Bizarre/Straight

One of Zappa's most original moves was to set up his own label long before The Beatles founded Apple. Zappa did not just guarantee his own artistic and financial independence, but also promoted other artists. They were all virtually unknown, but some were even given the opportunity to record double albums (Beefheart, Lenny Bruce, Wildman Fischer). The label catered for differing tastes, literally from the bizarre to the straight. The albums were always packaged

in superb sleeves by 'graphic engineer' Cal Schenkel, who also designed The Mothers' covers. Cal now lives in Pennsylvania.

At Zappa's side, running the label and working as manager was Herb Cohen, 'Master of Biznis'. Herb Cohen was born in 1933, and among his previous employment was working as an arms dealer in Africa helping Lumumba. Other jobs included fireman, representative of the Union of Stewards, and the army, which he soon left for reasons of 'incompatibility'. While in the army he became interested in folk music after seeing the singer Odetta. He emigrated to L.A., and from 1956 ran a club called The Purple Onion.

Among the artists who appeared at the club were Brownie McGee, Sonny Terry and a certain Theodore Bikel *('200 Motels')*. Cohen helped run various other venues in L.A. and in 1959, at Cosmo Alley, met a young comedian, Lenny Bruce. On moving to Hollywood he met Frank Zappa. The two worked together until 1976 when Frank gave his manager a declaration of independence because he felt Cohen had taken too many liberties while running the labels Bizarre, Straight and especially Discreet, and left too much of the organizing to his lawyer brother Mutt.

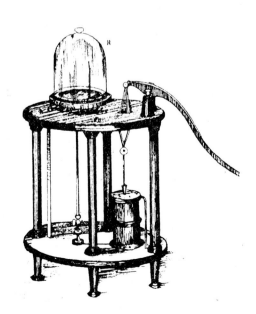

It was a fine adventure while it lasted. While co-running Zappa's label, Cohen often had to deal with several tricky customers as well as cater to big companies and attend to the wishes of artists as awkward and unconventional as Beefheart.

Cohen says: "For 'Trout Mask Replica' Zappa said to Beefheart, 'Go into the studio, rehearse as much as you need, and we'll do it how you want'. It was the first album that Beefheart could do under his own control, taking instructions from nobody. Frank called me one day and said that Beefheart was up at the house and needed some help. So I got him round to the office and he sat down. First it took us six months to get him out of the legal entanglements he was in. He had some extravagant ideas. Like, he wanted an extra 800 dollars added to his budget to pay for a tree surgeon. He said that as he practised outside, he wanted to be sure that the vibrations from his amps wouldn't make the leaves fall off the branches of a tree in front of the house. I suggested he should move his amps around to face the other way. Another time Beefheart told me the equipment he'd be needing, and asked for twenty sets of sleigh bells. I asked him why, because I knew that in the studio there were only five musicians, one producer and one engineer, and even if they all used two hands, they'd only need fourteen. He said, 'We're going to overdub them!'".

Wild Man Fischer

In a different genre from Beefheart, Fischer is also an individual case. Today he is still struggling along on Rhino Records making albums on which he insults Zappa. Cohen remembers: "That guy was singing on the streets. You've heard accusations that he was ripped off? Oh yeah, well he's totally out of his mind. See, it was not exactly what you'd call a successful album. I don't think we sold more than 7000 copies and Frank had been in the studios with the guy for three months. But Fischer's an unfortunate victim of the culture. He'd been committed to institutions a couple of times, and the last time he beat up his mother. They threatened to put him away again, and so he disappeared. Unfortunately you can't deal with him on any kind of logical basis. He got paid for doing it though. He got money and so forth. I never paid him large sums, but what we did do was pay him every week for a long period of time. And the point is, whatever you paid him, it was gone the next day, so we tried to pay him money in small doses. What we did was put

him on a salary and put him in hotels. And, you know, Bizarre/Straight was not as rich as Columbia or Warner/Kinney."

Sound Engineers

Zappa's career really started to take off when he bought Paul Buff's studio and founded Studio Z. It was unique, for while many of those around him were still becoming used to stereo sound, Buff left Zappa a 5-track studio. Paul Buff used to play every instrument himself, using overdubs and he perfected a way of recording on to acetate demo-discs in place of cassettes. The problem was that acetate discs were easily damaged by dust and were highly inflammable. Because of this, a vacuum cleaner was vital for when Zappa and Buff took the acetates to record companies! Beefheart holds one such appliance on the inner cover of 'Hot Rats'. From time to time Zappa and Buff would set fire to stacks of old acetates at night, lighting up the whole neighbourhood. This inspired the vacuum cleaner stories on 'Chunga's Revenge' and 'The Perfect Stranger'.

A few years later, while recording 'We're Only In It For The Money' and 'Lumpy Gravy', Zappa called in Gary Kellgren (who can be seen on the cut-out panel of 'We're...') because he was having problems with Capitol's recording engineers. They were used to recording drums one day, bass the next and so on, without working according to a set time-table, changing from one instrument to another and setting them together immediately. Gary Kellgren was the undisputed master of the rare 8-track studios at Mayfair, New York, and had recently worked with Jimi Hendrix. It was tricky for him because Zappa did not tell him which piece of tape corresponded to which instrument, so he had to familiarize himself with all the compositions, dissecting them bar by bar. Later, he said: "It made me better at it!" Since then, Kellgren has been working at the Record Plant, and lives opposite Herb Cohen.

Today, Zappa still works surrounded by electrician friends, some of whom have made him prototype special effects, like the Blue Box, a 48cm effects rack invented by Claus Wiedeman. As Frank often uses no lead for his guitar, the signal is transmitted by much the same system as a wireless mike. At the most extreme distances, in large concert halls, no loss or degradation of signal has been experienced. The signal is received by a pedal board, used to select the desired effect

or combination of effects, and is then sent to the Blue Box and split into four independently controlled signals which are met with buffer amps to maintain signal integrity. The signal

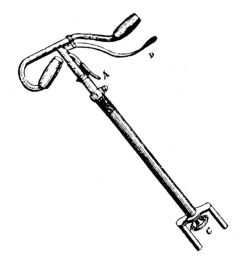

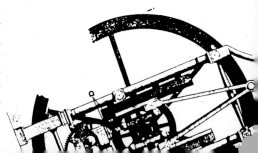

FZ and Herb Cohen at Midem, 1970.

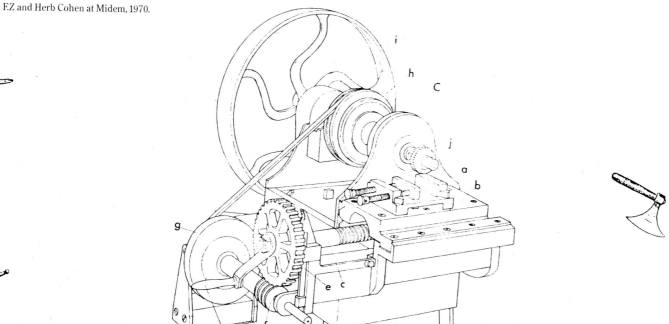

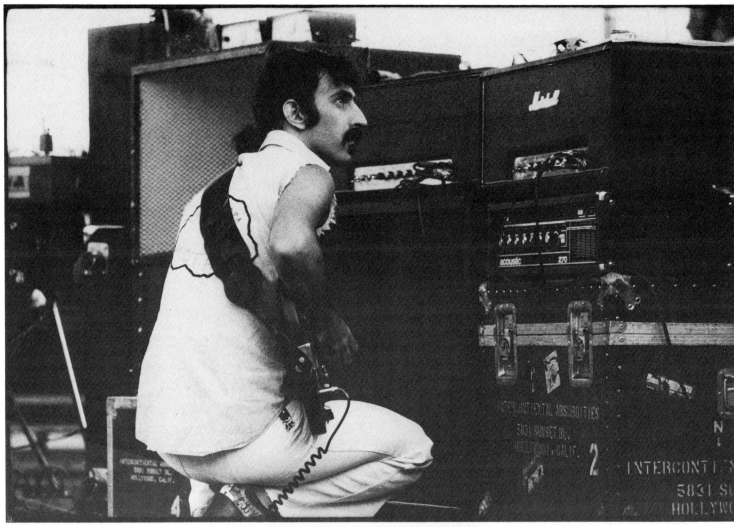

is then sent to an Alembic pre-amp for the appropriate routing to the special effects module. Not unlike other equipment used by Frank, this has been modified to include one additional effect: a Harmonizer. The effects used in the Blue Box are: MXR, Digital Delay, Big Muff Distortion, Space Echo, Eventide harmonzier, Bi-Phase and DBX Compression. These elements were modified by David Gray. They are all interfaced with other units in a jump loop, with the signal waiting at each module so as to respond readily to the relay switching employed. The signal finally arrives at a Yamaha 4 X mixing console, with an input for vocal mikes which allows special effects to be used on the voice, as well as an equalizer. The amplification is assured by a Mesa-Boogie and goes on through the Marshalls. Drums, percussion and keyboards are mixed onstage during the sound-check by the engineer and musicians. Every instrument with more than one input is mixed in stereo. Davey Moire handles the mixing and has two Yamaha PII 000s which are also modified.

Recently, Zappa has acquired a Carvin mobile studio, called the Utility Muffin Research Kitchen Remote Portable Studio, with a video console. This will probably replace the venerable Scully, but as he tours less these days, he sometimes lends it to Stevie Wonder. His latest acquisition is a Sony PCM portable studio, digital with 24 tracks. More work ahead for Thomas Nordegg.

Zappa's latest whizz-kid soundman is Mark Pinske, who is responsible for the excellent recording of his work with the London Symphony Orchestra, despite the cavernous size of the Twickenham studios. The equipment used was a Calrec, recording on 4 tracks, and several microphones – PZM, AKG 452 and D12. Outside the hall, two Sony OCM 3324s worked simultaneously.

Mark likes working with Zappa: "I've learnt a lot with him, he's a real master of montage techniques, in the way he edits the tapes to mix live and studio work, like a collage, even on digital. He's unique. With Frank I have to stay really alert. He's always looking for new techniques to try out. You've only just got used to one recording technique when he comes up with another equally unconventional one. I've learnt four times as much with him as I did at school".

The LSO project was not the most complex task for Mark Pinska. The New York concert on Halloween night, transmitted by satellite, was tough in a different way: "I had to get everything working together. We had six interfaced cameras and we were mixing both in stereo for ourselves, and in mono for the TV".

Mark Pinska reckons it is harder to be a good sound engineer in rock than it is in classical music, especially if you are working with people like Zappa and he cites as proof Bob Auger, who began working with The Kinks and today works for Boulez.

The Zappa Concern

Frank Zappa is at the head of a full-scale enterprise and, like any other, it has its budget. Over the last five years he has spent $500,000 having his music copied and printed. The LSO project cost $300,000, the cancelled concert with the Viennese Symphony Orchestra cost $125,000, including phone bills, hotels and music publishing, and he never received the $300,000 promised by Austrian TV. The salary of an American musician at the Dutch festival is estimated to be $15,000 for seventeen weeks in Europe. Each album Zappa makes costs between $60,000 and $100,000, excluding the musicians who receive an annual wage. Zappa's staff includes Bruce Brickford, the animator of modelling clay, house copyists like Steve Vai who works as a transcriber, two permanently salaried electricians David Ocker and Steve Di Furia who work at programming the Synclavier computer, soundsmen Mark Pinska, Bob Stone and Thomas Nordegg.

There is also ex-Mother Arthur Barrow who works as rehearsal guide to new musicians joining the band, as well as the Barking Pumpkin label with its complete secretariat, and its subsidiary New Age Art, the graphics concern.

Before touring, Zappa uses his rehearsal room fully equipped. The material then goes on to the articulated trucks, and the band of seven or eight musicians leave with the roadies, sound engineer, lighting people and road managers. There is also the pressing factory, which works principally for Zappa, with John Matousek at its head.

Last, but not least, there is his studio at home, the UMRK centre which used to be called The Basement, Dr Zircon's Secret Lab in Happy Valley.

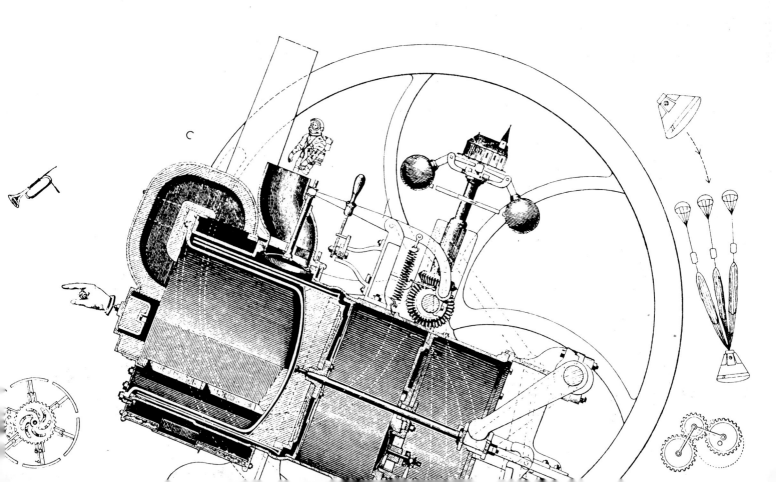

4

ZAPPA'S MUSICAL tHEatRe

Many are the critics who have commented on Zappa's work. All too often self-appointed social moralists and armchair critics hungry for an instantly aesthetic gratification have misled themselves by carping at individual details in his lyrics, forgetting to observe them with the attention they deserve in the wider context of his music as a whole. Because of this, Zappa's words have often been strongly criticised both for their crudeness and their articulate obscurity. Yet these words are a means of initiation into the Zappa universe, and both describe the bizarre but strongly drawn characters (Uncle Meat, Billy The Mountain, Greggery Peccary), and support the action by reflecting the different episodes in their extravagant adventures.

The music also has a vital role in structuring the story, and animates the characters, their thoughts and actions. Scene setting and dialogue can also be absorbed into a musical framework. 'Them Or Us' (the book) is unique as it gives an overall view of his base concepts on the same thematic material, and their different expressions over the years, like a musical diary. From the early days at the dawn of the sixties up to his most recent material, Zappa's work has been in constant evolution. This is the saga of Zappa. This perpetual change, and the massive amount of detail it contains, is spread over numerous musical and lyrical themes that exist outside the individual albums and are constantly renewed. It is a fascinating process. Details, symbols and cross references resonate through his complete works and are set in a wide variety of contexts. While some of the more topical themes are left behind with their era, others that might seem insignificant at first develop out of all proportion as if he had only later discovered new musical and lyrical uses for them.

Zappa is exceptional in that he can look back over his prolific complete works and give it new perspectives and meanings, as he does in 'Them Or Us' (the book). On some albums it is clearly the sound of the music which is the centre of interest; on others both words and music are so tightly interwoven that both vie for the listener's interest; while on others the words dominate with the music in a supportive role. There can be no doubt as to Zappa's lyrical originality and these make important contributions to his rich network of allusions and internal relationships, as well as describing situations and depicting characters.

The precision with which he creates and animates the symbols, motifs, cross-

references and minute details that make up his ever expanding body of work is impressive, especially as throughout this perpetual transformation he has kept a musical style which defies critical attempts to push it into one particular form (pop, jazz, modern orchestral, film etc). Zappa regards this sort of categorisation as absurd, unnecessary and archaic. It exists in contradiction to the versatile fluidity his music represents.

In music the term for this is the German word 'leitmotive', and it is this versatility which charges the recurrent themes with new power, for their transformation depends on the exact moment they are used, and the reasons for which they are included. There is never any indecision and Zappa knows perfectly well how they need to be adapted, and often appears to enjoy finding new variations, modifying the tempo or the intervals in the melody. For example, the theme from 'Black Page' ('In New York') can be found reworked and adapted without being unrecognizable in numerous other compositions. In 'Bogus Pomp' and 'Pedro's Dowry', there are shortened, barely recognizable snippets from '200 Motels'. In the series of movements that make up 'Moe's Herb Vacation', it is virtually impossible to link the work to some pre-existing, easily defined form. Some music critics have complained that it is 'formless' and that it just consists of a series of moments, but it is music that demands a different sort of attitude from the listener if he or she wishes to understand the original ideas by which Zappa has constructed his piece. Necessity is, after all, the mother of invention.

This way of listening implies that such works are non-limited constructions which only stop expanding provisionally. Nothing is concluded and there are further possibilities for development. Over the years, Zappa has cultivated the contrast between extremely coherent albums ('We're Only In It For The Money', 'Apostrophe', 'Overnite Sensation', 'One Size Fits All', 'Joe's Garage', 'Thingfish') and albums on which his approaches to composition are deliberately varied ('Burnt Weeny Sandwich', 'Man From Utopia', 'Them Or Us').

Zappa is remarkable for his tireless drive to experiment and has used numerous bands and orchestras to provide a distinctive richness and complexity of instrumentation that runs through his original adaptations of different styles. His arrangements are very realistic and often shape diverse, even conflicting, elements into an intense musical relationship, but the abundant imagination is

strictly calculated and worked out in incredibly minute detail.

"What I'm trying to describe is the type of attention given to each lyric, melody, arrangement, improvisation, the sequence of these elements in an album, the cover art which is an extension of the musical material, the choice of what is recorded, released and/or performed during a concert, the continuity or contrast from album to album, etc...etc... All these detail aspects are part of the Big Structure or The Main Body Of Work. The smaller details comprise not only the contents of The Main Body Of Work, but, because of the chronology of execution, give it a 'shape' in an abstract sense." (From '200 Motels' booklet).

Michael H. Kenyon, 30, the suspected enema bandit who terrorized coeds at the University of Illinois for 10 years, has pleaded guilty in Urbana, Ill., to six counts of armed robbery. He has admitted administering enemas to woman victims in at least three of the six robberies.

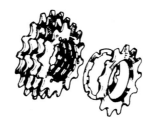

"Everyone should have a gas mask at home," F.Z.

Some take such statements as evidence of a fixed plan, others mistake the humour for a composer's vanity, but in Zappa's music everything is intentional. If we imagine, as he suggests (also in the '200 Motels' booklet) the head of a pin "containing an amazingly detailed illustration of some sort... Now, imagine that it's not a pin...it's a musical note with a corresponding physical action". These pins can be accumulated on, say, a map of North America as shown on the 'Uncle Meat' cover, or on a zodiac like the one on 'One Size Fits All'. The collection of these pins and the pattern of their layout is the album, what Zappa calls a 'basic unity'. The same logic can be applied to individual albums in the context of the complete works. Each one is an intricately detailed design, contributing to the overall pattern and, says Zappa, "Whether you can imagine it or not, that's what the deal is".

As can be seen, despite its constant reworkings, Zappa's music is far from being turned in on itself, infinitely recycling its own inventions like some grotesque intellectual fungus. When looking back over his musical output, it becomes clear that the entire musical history of the second part of the twentieth century is passing before our eyes: greedy and sinister governments, victims of dangerous obsessions (like the incestuous father in 'Magdalena'), the leather brigade ('Crew Slut'), pseudo oriental cosmic debris ('Apostrophe'), religious sects run by criminals ('Joe's Garage', 'Thingfish'), naivete of adolescents manipulated by cynical fashion business ('Flower Punk' from 'We're Only In It...' or 'I'm So Cute' from 'Sheik Yerbouti'). Groupies, touring, disco and much, much more all go to make up Zappa's human comedy of the modern world; this is the saga of Zappa. He is both a musician and social critic, and not primarily a satirist as some have claimed. The reason he composes is for music, his music. "Music is the best". He writes it seriously: "You know, I don't just go to work and say, 'I'll now make a satire of this'. I start writing and that's what comes out. I'm not specifically a satire person. I'm a composer with a sense of humour".

An overall plan gradually emerges from this network of lyrics, solos, and cross references as many enigmas are resolved in the alchemy of word and sound. This strange puzzle, destined to remain obscure for those who only listen with half an ear, is renewed as album follows album. It both generates the 'conceptual continuity', and has attracted a large number of listeners, a collection of people as large, unconditional and varied as Zappa's music. This has become known as The Brotherhood Of Zappa or The Zappaphiles.

Several years after being Cucamonga's eccentric, he says: "Look, I was just a creepy guy from San Diego playing weird music thought to have no commercial potential. Here it is thirteen years and a few dozen albums later. I've got a hot little disco number sizzling on the charts, a couple of lawsuits sizzling in the courts, I live in Hollywood, my music is still bizarre and I look exactly the same. So who's weird?"

This acknowledgement is his revenge on the difficult years behind him, for Zappa has consistently managed to prove that his music does have commercial potential, and this has demanded immense patience, extraordinary energy and a work schedule that spans years,

made up of albums that clamour to be heard. Zappa is an unrelenting worker and a committed craftsman. He has carved out his empire completely without compromise, and he reacts angrily when people try to turn his music to their own profit. He has no desire to end his days in poverty and oblivion like the venerated Varèse, or in a state of insanity with just a guitar like his hero in 'Joe's Garage'. He is much better off as a legend, especially a living one.

"The present day composers refuse to die." Edgar Varèse.

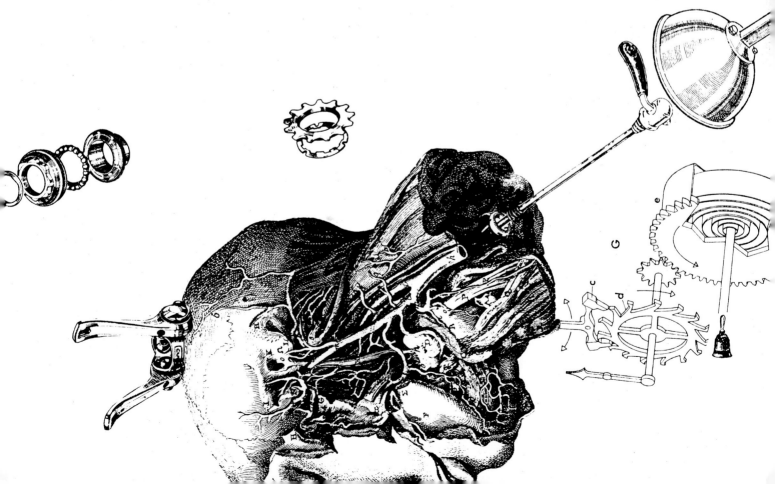

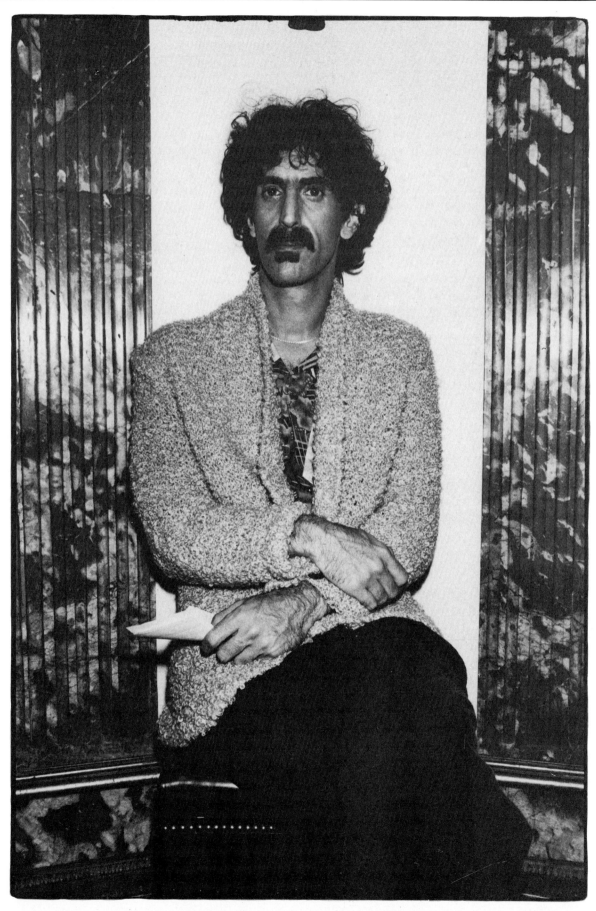

5

NO COMMERCIAL POTENTIAL.

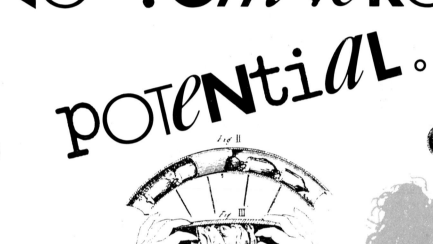

a CRitiCal DiSCOgraPHY

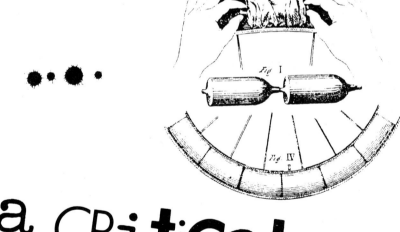

Throughout Zappa's complete works, one album reflects another in a variety of ways (the famous Conceptual Continuity). In this chapter, all of his officially released material is examined under a critical spotlight. This is not intended to be negative or destructive, more a glorification of these wonderful and often legendary recordings.

Freak Out, 1966

This album was recorded on a four track tape machine, which makes it a technical feat in itself. It was also, along with Dylan's 'Blonde On Blonde', the only noteworthy double LP of its time to include long compositions taking up the whole of a side. Its musical construction (blending electronic effects, popular music and classically influenced arrangements) was barely tolerated, let alone considered commercially acceptable until The Beatles' 'Sgt. Pepper' about a year later. Despite its lack of instant commercial potential, 'Freak Out' made waves among those who bothered to listen. In 'Return Of The Son Of Monster Magnet', which is influenced by Edgar Varèse, snatches of conversation, onomatopoeic noises, shouts and squeaks are combined with a siren and a set piano part, and finally disintegrate into the speeded up, high pitched voice of a cartoon character. 'Help, I'm A Rock' (later covered by the psychedelic group, The West Coast Pop Experimental Band) is a genuine piece of music as director Julian Beck's The Living Theatre, with its succession of sounds, orgasmic cries and mockery aimed at the police.

'Freak Out' is above all a social comment on America in the mid-1960s, which derides radio plugging ('Brain Police') and chirpy teenage love pap('Go Cry On Somebody Else's Shoulder') and speaks of the race riots in Watts in 1965 ('Trouble Every Day'). Amid the bland silliness of much of its contemporaneous music, 'Freak Out' stands out as a violent criticism of the modern environment, and combines lyrical extremism with both musical nostalgia and experimentation to form a Theatre Of The Absurd, reflecting the absurdity of the 'American way of life' in a disturbing state of cultural decomposition.

Absolutely Free, 1966

'Absolutely Free' continues the social comment that began on 'Freak Out', but is even more virulent, denouncing the American way of life and caricaturing the

stupidity of 'Plastic People'. The raw, derisive vocals are tough and raunchy, sometimes grating at the extreme edges of tunefulness. Throughout the album this aggressive approach is pitted against Byrdish balladry, and there is a constant and provocative collage effect in the unexpected changes between different sorts of music. On 'Brown Shoes Don't Make It' there are snatches of dodecaphonic scales, ballads, rock, R&B, Beach Boys, soap opera and more, and the contrast between these different styles creates some previously

unimaginable effects, and ensures that this is no piece of easy listening. On 'Plastic People' a clarinet plays several bars from Stravinsky's 'Rite Of Spring', and this composer's influence runs deep throughout the album, especially on 'Amnesia Vivace' (clarinet and voice), 'Status Back Baby' and 'Call Any Vegetable'. The last track, 'America Drinks And Goes Home', a parody of an old-time dance band in a smooth hotel bar, is a fox-trot with Mingus style blues (from 'Passions Of A Man', from the LP 'Oh Yeah!') set against a rising background of cash-register noises, conversation, shouts and breaking glass. On 'Absolutely Free' Zappa strips musical beauty of previously hallowed definitions, chops it up, polishes it, and creates a new sound-world which is grandiose, surrealist and slightly obscene, all in accordance with his vision.

Lumpy Gravy, 1967

This is Zappa's first fully symphonic effort, and is both one of his most mythical albums and the one that sold the least. Its release suffered lengthy delays because of quarrelling between MGM and Capitol. 'Lumpy Gravy' enabled Zappa to turn his taste for orchestral composition in general, and contemporary electro-acoustic work in particular, into an album. The LP takes the listener into the modern classical universe of Stockhausen ('Kontakte'), John Cage ('Variations For Piano'), Varèse ('Deserts') and Satie, which makes it a veritable initiation ceremony for the pop public. There are also touches of film music ('Chrome Plated Megaphone'), splashes of Dixieland and a part reminiscent of Wild Man Fischer ('Merry Go Round').

Although the arrangements are not always as polished as they could be, the musical themes immediately grab the attention, and many of them resurface, transformed by Zappa's alchemy, on later albums. Details, musical quotations, fleeting hints and ideas sketched out on 'Lumpy Gravy' can be found on 'Oh No!' ('Weasels Ripped My Flesh'), 'Chrome Plated Megaphone' ('We're Only In It For The Money'), 'King Kong' ('Uncle Meat') and 'Redneck Eats' ('200 Motels'). 'The Finale', later covered by Gruppo Sportivo, becomes 'Take Your Clothes Off When You Dance'. This was subsequently reworked to form parts of 'Greggery Peccary' and 'Redunzl'.

We're Only In It For The Money, 1967

Middle class American youth fell in step with The Beatles and turned hungry for Indian gurus, occult sciences and psychedelic visions. Zappa remained dissatisfied with the whole Flower Power mythology, regarding its beatific attitudes both as a new manifestation of his generation's stupid naïvete, and a conspiracy by those in power: "Despite their clothes, most young Americans still think the same way as their parents and have merely adopted the old prejudices and stupidities in a different wrapping." (Actuel No.3).

After a series of devastating concerts with The Fugs, and after asking an unsmiling Paul McCartney for permission to parody the 'Sgt. Pepper' sleeve, Zappa brought out 'We're Only In It For The Money', an allusion to the fortune that The Beatles were making from their hippyish new look. It is a bitter, funny, sometimes even cruel criticism of the miserable daily lives of hippies and their lost youth (*'Flower Punk'*), as well as ballads with sinister and political themes (*'Mom and Dad'*, *'The Idiot Bastard Son'*). The careful use of contrasts, ruptures and tape loops makes it one of Zappa's best studio tapes ever, and there is wide use of backwards tape, overdubbing and other electro-acoustic effects. An intricate and subtle album that has lost none of its dynamic freshness.

Ruben And The Jets, 1967

"Is this the Mothers Of Invention recording under a different name in an attempt to get their cruddy music on radio?" asks the sleeve, but this is much more than a collection of smoothie clichés, despite the brilliantly cretinous lyrics. It captures the authentic sound of a bunch of old-time rock and rollers recreating the good old days in the studio.

Zappa loves this music which rocked his adolescence in the 1950s and clearly enjoys playing sounds like the ones that turned him on at High School. He has frequently said that he could happily write hundreds of songs in this style.

'Ruben And The Jets' is a pause in Zappa's musical evolution, but beneath the sugary melodies there still lurks a criticism of American society and cheap teenage love. This is one of his indispensable albums and you will still be listening to it in twenty years time when other nostalgicists are trying to recreate the good old days of Zappa, The Doors and Hendrix, or even The Police and The Eurythmics!

Uncle Meat, 1968

'Uncle Meat' is a concept album and shows Zappa as the undisputed Fu-Manchu of popular music. It is a surrealistic collage in which absurdity and nonsense rub shoulders with experimental, classical and baroque music, plus generous helpings of free-jazz and slices of conversation from every-day life (*'Voice of Suzy Creamcheese'*, *'Our Bizarre Relationship'*). All is united by the idea of *'The Big Note'*, which is instantly recognizable to anyone who knows their Zappa, for it is a term applied to his characteristic obsessions, mannerisms and other distinguishing marks that make his music immediately identifiable. On *'Uncle Meat'* it is represented by the percussion, especially the marimbas.

The title track is a short piece for harpsichord and percussion which has much quirky charm, and follows the disintegrating boogie of *'Nine Types Of Industrial Pollution'*, reminiscent of Varèse's *'Ionisation'*. Zappa has always appreciated Stravinsky's music and enjoys composing in this style, as can be seen from *'Uncle Meat Variations'*, *'Zolar Czakl'* and *'Dog Breath'*. *'King Kong'*, the album's *pièce de résistance* is a long jazzy suite containing superb solos by two of the legendary Mk 1 Mothers, Bunk Gardner on sax and Don Preston on piano. *'Project X'* sounds like an early experimental draft of *'Black Page'*, while *'Prelude To King Kong'* is an undisguised tribute to Albert Ayler.

"This is a group of eight musicians who can play all kinds of music (Varèse, Stockhausen, Ornette Coleman, The Beatles, Fanfare music, Shopp, traditional jazz), and still succeed in establishing their own musical identity, using all kinds of jokes, gimmicks and skills at their disposal in the studio. Popularity, synthesis, the power both to charm and to shock – perhaps Zappa's work in Sun Ra's dream made real."
(Philippe Carles. Translated from *Jazz Magazine* No. 161.)

Hot Rats, 1969

'Hot Rats' is a complete break with the on-stage theatrical eccentricities and improvised musical happenings of previous records. Here all is kept under tight control from start to finish, leaving no room for free-jazz frenzy. This album is daring in a different way in that it is one of the first to give rock and jazz a real classical edge that is reminiscent of chamber music. It is less provocative but more seductive as a result of the abundantly rich instrumentation and intense mixing work in the studio. The arrangements are neither strident nor flashy, but have a lavish magnificence in 'Peaches En Regalia', and 'Song Of Mr Green Genes', and an exotic lushness in 'Little Umbrellas'.

By this album Zappa had disbanded the original Mothers and was primarily working with jazz musicians (Ponty) and bluesmen (Shuggy Otis and Sugarcane Harris), who gave his band a new level of technical proficiency. 'Hot Rats' is above all the result of a close and fruitful collaboration between Zappa and Ian Underwood, who profits from this opportunity to show off his talents as a pianist. Underwood's contributions to this LP are remarkable, especially the sax solo on 'Gumbo Variations' – he is a multi instrumentalist – in which he tips his hat to Sonny Rollins.

'Willie The Pimp', the longest track, features verses sung by Don Vliet (Captain Beefheart) and an endless Zappa guitar solo. In his book on Zappa, Alain Dister quotes Phil Manzanera (ex-Roxy Music) as saying: "His solo on 'Willie The Pimp' seems to go on forever. I tried playing along to the original but had to stop, exhausted. Zappa has doubled the number of notes in an octave a guitarist can play. He adds fifths and ninths to make it sound almost smooth, then adds wah-wah to stop it becoming too much so."

Burnt Weeny Sandwich, 1969

On 'Burnt Weeny Sandwich' Zappa serves up old material recorded before the dissolution of the original Mothers, worn out by years of touring. This is intended to fill in on the history of the group and is the first album not united by one musical or aesthetic concept. Yet, it is far from being a mess of stale left-overs, and no dead horses are flogged here. The 'Hunchback Suite', a favourite piece of The Mothers Mk 1, is particularly notable, and appears under the title 'The Little House I Used To Live In'. It opens with a beautifully muted piano solo from Ian Underwood, reminiscent in style of Debussy's 'Preludes'. After an electric fanfare (Zappa has a marked taste for fanfares) it slips into a jazzy tempo, over which Sugarcane Harris turns in what is perhaps his best ever violin solo, full of modernistic runs and counterpoints, offset by Don Preston on piano. After a brief baroque interlude, Zappa himself contributes incisive organ parts that polish it off in fine style. Side one contains two tributes to Igor Stravinsky between 'Holiday In Berlin' and 'Berlin Full Blown', fanfare based music inspired by the extreme left wing unrest in Berlin 1968. On the title track Zappa plays one of the most subtle guitar solos of his entire career.

But after playing the festival at Amougies, Zappa was already heading in new directions…

Weasels Ripped My Flesh, 1970

This is a second collection of older material, following on from 'Sandwich', and is one of Zappa's most aggressively bizarre works, full of cross references to free-jazz and modern classical musicians such as Berio. Roy Estrada's mighty guffaws and the deliberately exaggerated singing of Lowell George, who later formed Little Feat, are a slight parody of Cathy Berberian. Estrada's shout-laughing led to a film of The Mothers being banned from French television in 1968.

'Toads Of The Short Forest' is hardly less cacophonous, with Art Tripp, playing drums in 7/8 time, Jim Black on timpani in 3/4, Estrada on bass in 3/4, Don Preston on piano in 5/8, and a tambourine in 3/4, while the alto saxophonist "blows his nose". Don Preston shows that he is a master of electronic effects on this LP, especially in 'Dwarf Nebula', but the best piece here is undoubtedly 'Eric Dolphy Memorial Barbecue'. "The cleverest tribute that could have been paid to him, it summarizes this great saxophonist's contributions, and shows that they have been clearly understood." (From J.P. Patillot in Jazz Hot.)

A long page of Mothers' history is definitively turned with this album. Those nostalgic for this period will have to be content with their memories.

Chunga's Revenge, 1970

At about the time he met Ponty, Zappa also got to know George Duke, who gradually became a pillar of the new Mothers, as did drummer Aynsley Dunbar (ex-John Mayall's Bluesbreakers), whom Zappa met at Amougies. The subsequent arrival of ex-Turtles Mark Volman and Howard Kaylan completed the new group, which was much more conventional and less geared to experimentation than the earlier Mothers. The sound here is more rock; the lyrics are mostly rock satire, and less directly critical of American society. For example, 'Road Ladies' gives a disenchanted view of a rock band on tour with 'no-one but groupies and promoters to love you, and a pile of laundry by the motel door'. This looks ahead to the themes of '200 Motels'.

This is a rather transitory album featuring Zappa on harpsichord and George Duke playing Gillespie style scats on 'The Nancy And Mary Music'. Zappa plays hot guitar on 'Transylvania Boogie', which is perhaps his equivalent of Larry Coryell's 'Elementary Guitar Solo'. The title track, 'Chunga's Revenge', deserves special mention because Ian Underwood's use of alto and plus wah-wah is reminiscent of Miles Davis.

'Chunga's Revenge' also features the vacuum cleaner which resurfaces fourteen years later on 'The Perfect Stranger'.

Fillmore East, June 1971

This rather poorly recorded album marks the debut of Flo and Eddie, stage names of the two ex-Turtles, who get the lion's share here with long dialogues, supported by Zappa, on the subject of the daily lives of rock stars and their opposite numbers, the groupies. It is a link between the rougher sound of 'Chunga's Revenge' and the maturity of '200 Motels'. This is Zappa's first live album, a shortened version of the Fillmore show, and opens with a rock version of 'Little House' which becomes the signature tune for the concert's title, 'Mudshark'. This is introduced by Zappa over a bluesy tempo, which occasionally flirts with gospel, before returning to 'Little House' on guitar and keyboards. Mark Volman and Howard Kaylan poke fun at Alice Cooper and 'Late Solar Beef' is ornamented with allusions to 'The Turkish March'. 'Willie The Pimp' (Part 2), has a heavy, saturated sound reminiscent of The Stooges. 'Do You Like My New Car?' is another star-meets-groupie story with references to Three Dog Night, David Cassidy, The Monkees and more.

This is a small scale Zappa theatre that many found less appealing despite some high points. But Zappa's distinctive sense of humour was about to find a fresh musical expression in '200 Motels'.

Each night at the Fillmore, Zappa gave the concert a comical theme depending on the wishes of the audience, the band or his own ideas.

200 Motels, 1971

'200 Motels', Zappa's self-reflecting monumental construction, was primarily a film with a $600,000 budget, shot first on video and then transferred to 35mm. It was no slapstick pop musical or live concert footage, but a surrealistic documentary, a report on real events and an extrapolation from them. It tells of the life of a band on the road and draws on contact with the audience, the internal chemistry of the group, classical music, and the group's relationship with groupies.

This double album is not really a soundtrack to the film, as some of the film music does not appear on it and vice versa. Instead Zappa adopts the approach of those film musicians who were among the few to have made systematic use of discoveries made by musicians earlier this century (Varèse, Stravinsky, Schoenberg). Zappa had already written the music to the films Run Home Slow and The World's Greatest Sinner around 1959/60, and his use of cellos on 'Touring Can Make You Crazy' is reminiscent of Bernard Hermann in The Mysterious Island or Jason And The Argonauts, while 'Dance Of The Just Plain Folks' and 'Lucy's Seduction' are remarkable resumés of film music technique.

There is Penderecki influence in 'This Town Is A Sealed Tuna Sandwich', and echoes of Ligeti in 'Mysterioso', and of Webern in 'Nun Suit'. 'Dental Hygiene Dilemma' and 'I'm Stealing The Towels' appear to have been inspired by the 'Ballet Mecanique' (1925), written by George Antheil, an early experimentalist, especially in percussion who, like Varèse, emigrated to the U.S.A.

To help make the film, Zappa brought in classical guitarist John Williams, Theodore Bikel, who is more accustomed to singing old Russian and Jewish melodies, Ringo Starr, who plays the part of Zappa, Keith Moon, who plays the part of a frustrated nun, and many more. Those who appreciated Zappa's music before this album liked it even more; those who did not despaired of him.

Just Another Band From L.A., 1972

This LP was a clutch of good-time live performances released by Zappa to remind everybody that he was still there, even though his leg was in plaster. Little new material is unveiled, but Zappa presents a sort of musical recreation, consisting mostly of rocked-up older pieces, spiced with Howard Kaylan's amusing candy-store melodies.

Though lacking onstage visual impact, '*Billy The Mountain*' is a successful and involved piece of musical theatre. Billy is a mountain who goes on vacation with his girlfriend Ethel, a tree. The government tries to draft him and sends in the would-be cool headed hero Studebaker Hawk. When it was released, some critics, like P. Paringaux in *Rock & Folk* 1971, grafted other characters on to the story: "Billy is a mammoth, an incredible monument to Zappa's prodigious imagination and talents as a composer". He tells of God who sits on his sofa suspended in the heavens smoking his cigar, entertained by angels, a girl and a pig, warning them not to dirty his sofa. Paringaux also mentions Zircon, who dances in a cave, leeches and giant fan-lights which devour anything that comes their way. Zircon creates Billy and Ethel, a tree-cum TV aerial.

Waka/Jawaka, 1972

Stuck in his wheelchair and unable to tour, Zappa came up with a mostly instrumental album, '*Waka/Jawaka*', a sort of '*Hot Rats*' part two, but with new musical directions. It is calm and clear, with long compositions for orchestra, sometimes consisting of about twenty musicians who often play in a sort of jazzy big-band style with superbly polished instrumentation. When it came out, some said, for reasons of their own, that it was a rather joyless, petrified sort of music. In fact, Zappa seemed to be moving towards a more elaborate sort of music, exploring and creating new landscapes of sound, colour and intensity.

The title track uses a smaller band, with excellent playing from Sal Marquez on muted trumpet, and Aynsley Dunbar who plays in a style unusual for him. There is a tremendous richness of sound, and Dunbar's drumming provides a solid, yet light rhythm, decorated and enlarged by his cymbals into constantly changing patterns. This is modern, anti-formalist orchestral/rock music, and Dunbar's developing maturity is revealed as another of Zappa's great musical assets.

The Grand Wazoo, 1972

Having proved his maturity on '*WakaJawaka*', Dunbar literally explodes all over this album, which is one of the most essential LPs in the whole Zappa catalogue. Dunbar had by now become one of Zappa's privileged accomplices, and it would be nearly four years before Zappa found a drummer of similar stature in Terry Bozzio.

'*The Grand Wazoo*' is a mythical battle between Mediocrites, who represents Musak, and Emperor Cletus, who has a force of 5,000 brass players to make up the air force, 5,000 percussionists in the artillery, 5000 players of all kinds of electronic instruments, and a chorus of 100,000 singers.

As might be expected, the album has a big-band sound, a sort of logical sequel to the previous one, but is totally original. Much of it is flamboyant, brilliantly crafted jazz and rock, supported by Dunbar's rhythms, that allows plenty of space for the top soloists to do their exquisite stuff for posterity before going back to studio session work.

This LP is one of the pinnacles in Zappa's career, and proof of continuity after '*Ruben*', '*Uncle Meat*', '*Zircon*' etc.

FZ, Howard Kaylan, Mark Volman,

Overnite Sensation, 1973

'Overnite' offers compact, punchy arrangements and funky – at times almost Stevie Wonderish – rhythms. It combines delirious, often erotic lyrics with intricate vocal and percussion parts. The musicianship is indisputably effective (Mr. and Mrs. Underwood, Duke, Ponty), and Zappa sings in a gruff and occasionally ironic tone.

This album was an immediate success almost everywhere and was vital in that it both pleased the older fans and attracted a whole new audience. Zappa was no longer a freak's legend but could communicate his visions to a generation used to more mainstream rock. From now on, with one or two exceptions (e.g. 'Zoot Allures'), Zappa's work, on stage and off, would be a synthesis of different Mothers' sounds, an effective introduction for his new listeners to the music of his earlier albums.

Apostrophe, 1974

The 'Apostrophe' sleeve says: "This is an album of songs and stories set to music performed for your dining and dancing pleasure," and it unites old friends such as Ray Collins, a first generation Mother, and Sugarcane Harris, with new ones like Napoleon Murphy Brock. There is also a distinguished guest, Jack Bruce. This crisp, perfectly controlled LP shows Zappa at one of the peaks of his popularity, and has some great moments: 'Stink Foot', 'Cosmik Debris', 'Nanook Rubs It'. On the title track, Jack Bruce displays his virtuosity without ostentation.

A niftily rock orientated album, on which Zappa bends his meticulous control of studio possibilities and the faultless technique of his musicians, to suit his fantasies. 'Apostrophe' is like an exercise in taking rock refinement to its logical extreme, before heading for new pastures.

Napoleon Murphy Brock, Chester Thompson, Ruth Underwood, Tom Fowler, Jeff Simmons, George Duke, Ralph Humphrey, F.Z, Bruce Fowler, 1973.

Roxy And Elsewhere, 1974

After widening his popularity with 'Overnite' and 'Apostrophe', Zappa went on tour, as much by taste as by necessity. He played Europe, too, which enabled him to celebrate ten years of performing in Paris. 'Roxy...' is a double live album of material from this period and is generally more successful than his previous live offerings. Featured are his old buddy Don Preston, Chester Thompson (Weather Report, Genesis), Napoleon Murphy Brock, George Duke and Ruth Underwood, who make up what is perhaps the best Mothers aggregation ever. The feel of the album is generally funky, but there are also older themes ('Son Of Orange County'), ballsy rock ('More Trouble Every Day'), ballads ('Village Of The Sun'), a jazz sketch ('Bebop Tango') and even a parody of Emerson, Lake and Palmer ('Edchina's Arf').

Each side has an introductory preamble which sometimes conjures up the atmosphere of Monster Movies, cartoons or lewd parables. Everything is kept under tight control, from Napoleon Murphy Brock's admirable soul voice to Ruth Underwood's virtuosity. It is hard to over-emphasise the importance of her contributions to The Mothers. George Duke supports them on keyboards and Zappa delivers some high class guitar work which ranges from Hendrix's domain to Santana, sometimes reworking older themes such as 'Oh No!' ('Weasels Ripped My Flesh').

The tracks here were the basis of the video show 'A Token Of His Extreme' which, far from being a nostalgic look-back over ten years of experience, showed Zappa's new directions which would find their best expression on Zappa's masterpiece 'One Size Fits All'.

F.Z Celebrates The Mothers tenth birthday in Paris.

One Size Fits All, 1975

During 1974 and 1975 Ruth Underwood, Murphy Brock and George Duke made up the best ever incarnation of The Mothers, and supported by such talented musicians Zappa really excelled himself on 'One Size Fits All'. The musicians were so versatile that he could pull out all the stops, and the album is almost a condensed history of his work, as well as offering new and exciting sounds. There is something for everyone here, and it is an excellent introduction to Zappa's music...one size, indeed, fits all!

The electronic effects that underlie 'Inca Roads' contain fleeting hints of '200 Motels', and the calm yet strong guitar solo, is at times reminiscent of 'Willie The Pimp' (Fillmore version) supported by a sparse bass riff. There are echoes of 'Lonesome Electric Turkey' (Fillmore). On 'Inca Roads' Ruth Underwood is particularly impressive and is well complemented by Duke in a complex musical dialogue that has its roots in 'Uncle Meat' and 'Waka/Jawaka' territory. 'Can't Afford No Shoes' is a blues piece typical of Canned Heat's style. 'Sofa' has a mock solemnity worthy of 'Hot Rats', and 'Po-jama People' is a humorous hunk of 'Apostrophe' style boogie with Duke on piano and a scorching guitar solo from Zappa.

'Florentine Pogen' combines music as diverse as 'Uncle Meat' and 'Ruben And The Jets' (the backing vocals) into an intricate mini-symphony, and is followed by 'Evelyn', a baroque puzzle. 'San Bernadino' is a superbly accomplished yet rough and ready boogie swagger, and 'Andy' is a philosophical sketch set to raunchy funk, with furious guitar work featuring Johnny Guitar Watson. With its brilliantly complex construction, internal coherence, constant inventiveness and consistently excellent lyricism, this album is a Zappa masterpiece, an indispensable crowning achievement to ten years of music.

Bongo Fury, 1976

This LP was a big disappointment after '*One Size Fits All*', but perhaps this is rather uncharitable as the album marks Zappa's reunion with Beefheart, who appears to have made amends for his past insults, judging by the sleeve. A victim of his own paranoia and thirst for success that seems to just elude him, Beefheart managed to fall out with even his most ardent defenders, his own musicians. Some of them went on to form Mallard.

After a few years of silence the Captain reappeared on this Zappa album in a starring role, and was given the chance to play several of his own compositions. His rugged voice is still effective and his harmonica playing is as good as ever, but throughout this record there is a distinct lack of punch. Neither really seem to give their all, as if they had few illusions about the doubtful stability of their reunion. '*Carolina Hardcore Ecstasy*' and '*Advance Romance*', a long blues work-out, are among the better tracks, but best of all is '*The Muffin Man*' which over the years has become a standard item of live encores.

Zoot Allures, 1976

Eyebrows were raised over this one, even among hard-core Zappaholics, while a younger generation of fans wondered whether this was the same Zappa who had made so many waves. Zappa's preoccupations appeared to be coldly aesthetic on this LP. Perhaps concerned by playing most of the instruments as well as working as sound engineer, Zappa seems to have forgotten to take both his sense of humour and provocative versatility into the studio with him. By trying to please himself as well as attract an audience more hungry for instantly consumable products than complex elaborate music, Zappa falls between two stools. Estrada appears and the standard of musicianship remains higher than many bands could hope for, but this must be one of his most resistible albums.

In New York, 1978

Rumours circulated among audiences: was Zappa becoming more interested in money than music? In fact, he was demanding money for tapes recorded but not paid for at Warner Bros. These were originally to come out as a boxed set made up of '*In New York*', '*Studio Tan*', '*Sleep-Dirt/Hot Rats No 3*' and '*Orchestral Favorites*'.

This album consists mainly of material that was played on the 1977 and 1978 European tours. It opens with '*Titties and Beer*', a dialogue between Zappa and Terry Bozzio (as the Devil), which although intriguing, does not carry the full impact of live visual effects. '*I Promise Not To Come In Your Mouth*' is a 'sensitive' synthesizer ballad, over which Eddie Jobson (ex-Roxy Music) played an excellent electric violin solo on the 1977 European tour. '*Big Leg Emma*' is a rather lacklustre cover of an old single, although '*Purple Lagoon/Approximate*', a long jazzy piece starring Mike Brecker on electric tenor sax, more than compensates for this.

The best side of this double album features '*Manx Needs Women*' and '*Black Page*', with a drum solo reminiscent of '*Project X*' ('*Uncle Meat*'). In its second part it turns into self parody with a distorted disco version and '*Illinois Enema Bandit*' brings it to a rousing finish. This album captures the feel of The Mothers live at different periods, and moves through a range of styles, from the first compositions of the early 1960s to the mid 1970s funky blues rhythms. It also has promise for the future.

Studio Tan, 1978

An album which suprised many who discovered Zappa with 'Apostrophe', and delighted those who favoured his earlier material. It is a move towards a more classico-contemporary style with a percussion base, which Zappa has always liked, and which was hinted at in 'Black Page'.

Side one tells of the many adventures of Greggery Peccary, a little pig who lives between Texas and Paraguay, and symbolises white collar middle America. One particularly entertaining moment is the scene in the stenopool at the mega-corporation 'Big Swifty & Associates'. Like 'Billy The Mountain', 'Greggery Peccary' is a musical film, almost a cartoon soundtrack, using diverse elements from throughout his work, reworked and rearranged into a new collage – a typical Zappa technique. Here we see traces of 'Lumpy Gravy', brief references to 'I'm Stealing The Towels' and 'Dental Hygiene Dilemma' (from '200 Motels'). The style of story-telling is similar to 'Billy The Mountain', and the band plays in a fashion that has its roots in 'The Grand Wazoo', while the bass in the background during the stenopool episode has been discreetly adapted from 'Carolina Hard Core Ecstasy' ('Bongo Fury'). Outside influences are Oliver Messaien, Pierre Boulez, and especially Spike Jones and Tex Avery.

Side two opens with 'Let Me Take You To The Beach', a sparkling parody of commercial pop. Next comes 'Music For Guitar And Low Budget Orchestra', a remake of a piece originally written for violin (Ponty), but improved by replacing Ponty's rather stilted style with Zappa's excellent fluid guitar. This new version is a remarkable synthesis of Zappa's music over the last eight years or so, as its introduction is an offspring of 'Twenty Small Cigars' ('Chunga's Revenge') followed by a guitar and piano duo which plays with themes from 'Little Umbrellas' and 'It Must Be A Camel' ('Hot Rats'). The central section is an arrangement of 'Music For Electric Violin' with touches of 'Waka/Jawaka'.

The last piece, 'Redunzl', contains a long Zappa guitar solo, full of inventiveness and energy, as well as a couple of cross references to the Ponty* album and 'Lumpy Gravy'. This wide-ranging album is Zappa's best since 'One Size Fits All', far beyond the perfunctory Zappa/Beefheart reunion or the flat disco-pop of 'Zoot Allures'.

* 'Ponty Plays The Music Of F. Zappa: King Kong'.

Sleep Dirt, 1979

Zappa bounces back in fine style after his legal problems. 'Live In New York' and 'Studio Tan' had already heralded this new energy and here he takes off his teenage clown costume and offers an album of striking maturity. Although released by Warner Bros, 'Sleep Dirt' is far from a bunch of old odds and ends. It is rigorous and demanding music, and for many will only start to sink in after repeated listenings. Zappa's renewed energy, far from loosening his compositional style, is remarkable for even greater seriousness, and under his tight control it blazes with an intensity that makes a lot of other music sound incredibly simple minded.

'Filthy Habits' is a beautiful, very luxuriant opener, whose modern classicism slips towards a courtly King Crimson-ish style, and even flirts with Black Sabbath (circa 'Paranoid') for a moment, before launching into a splendid two-part guitar solo. Part one echoes back to 'Transylvania Boogie' while the second part is reminiscent of 'Zoot Allures', and then subsides into a mass of electronic sound effects, which have not been used so cleverly since 'Electric Ladyland'.

'Flambay' begins by pretending to be muzak with jazzy bar-room piano and in its second part integrates dislocated tango and Irish jig rhythms. 'Regyptian Strut' appears to be written in the spirit of film music and side two opens with 'Time Is Money', which hovers at the limits of dodecaphonic music, proving as it does so that Maurizio Kagel was wrong and that popular and intelligent music can make excellent bedfellows. 'Sleep Dirt' (the track) is similar in style to 'Renés Theme', which sealed the reunion of Larry Coryell and John McLaughlin on the album 'Spaces'.

There are plentiful helpings of jazz-rock on this album, as well as experimentalism, which makes it a very fitting 'Hot Rats III'.

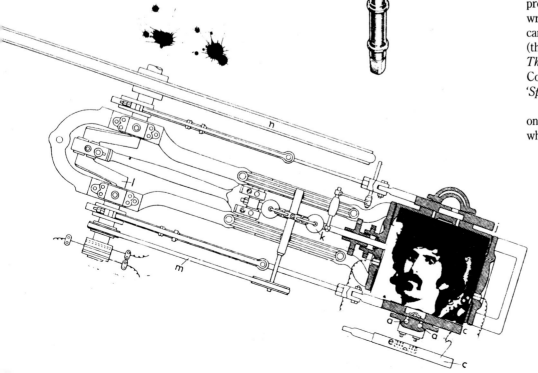

Sheik Yerbouti, 1979

Whether intentionally or not, Zappa is a master of paradox. After two years without a new album, Zappa heads suddenly got four in one year, two of them doubles! In the midst of lawsuits, a world tour and working on his next film *Baby Snakes*, he was still managing to move on to new developments that surprised everyone. *'Sheik Yerbouti'* was certainly a surprise to those who saw his last deliveries for Warner as 'sudden intellectualism'; it is a rocky, heavy album with kilos of energy invested in its four sides. It's hard to keep a straight face during the send-ups of Bob Dylan *('Flakes')* and Peter Frampton *('I've Been In You')*, or be left cold by the fire-breathing rhythms of *'Broken Hearts Are For Assholes'* and the savage, neo-punk thrash of *'I'm So Cute'*. Right on target Uncle Frank!

Zappa uses many styles on this album and varies through gospel-ish harmonies to fizzy funk *('City Of Tiny Lights')* through disco *('Dancing Fool')*, tango *('Yerbouti Tango')* and pieces for guitar solo *('Rat Tomago')*. There is also the admirable *'Bobby Brown'*: 'Oh God I am the American dream/ But now I smell like Vaseline/And I'm a miserable son of a bitch', as well as the excellent sleeve. In retrospect, this is the best response Zappa could have given to those who thought that a mere Punk 'revolution' would be enough to run him into a tired and boring old rock star. Some such young whippersnappers ran to the English rock weeklies to be told what 'modern' fashions they must adopt to best accentuate their acne, others thought this album was undeniable proof that Zappa was, and would remain, the best rock composer of present and future.

Orchestral Favorites, 1979

'Orchestral Favorites' rounds off the collection which was originally to come out as the boxed set *'Lather'* (pronounced 'leather'). 'In New York' was to present his live work, *'Studio Tan'* introduced musical theatre, *'Sleep Dirt'* showed his interest in experimenting with different musical fusions and *'Orchestral Favorites'* was to complete the picture with a selection of his compositions for orchestra.

'Strictly Genteel' is a version of the finale from *'200 Motels'* and retains a film music atmosphere. It is expansive and grandiose in style and structured by the contrast between plentiful reworkings from *'200 Motels'* and high-speed sound patterns that have their roots in *'Lumpy Gravy'*.

'Pedro's Dowry' moves through experimental-contemporary territory, and also contains droplets of *'Lumpy Gravy'*, as well as short sequences from *'Didja Get Any Onya?'* and *'Eric Dolphy Memorial Barbecue'* *('Weasels Ripped My Flesh')*. Are there fleeting glimpses of *'For Calvin'* *('Grand Wazoo')* and *'Uncle Meat'* *('Project X')?*

'Duke Of Prunes', originally on *'Absolutely Free'*, is given big-band treatment and *'Naval Aviation In Art'* has the shimmering surface of a Florentine optical illusion. *'Bogus Pomp'*, the most ambitious composition, mixes an astonishingly wide range of styles and includes reworkings from *'200 Motels'* such as *'The Sealed Tuna Bolero'* and *'This Town Is A Sealed Tuna Sandwich!'*

Some of those who discovered Zappa with *'Sheik Yerbouti'* must have been taken aback by this side of Zappa, but it showed that although he could plunder the entire history of rock and reinvent it his way, provide up to the minute social criticism and parody, and be one of rock's most creative guitarists, he never ceased to be an ambitious composer who wrote seriously (well, almost seriously!).

Joe's Garage, Act 1, 1979

Like a good wine, Zappa's work acquires a full bodied taste throughout his canon. The same year he released the excellent *'Sheik Yerbouti'* and *'Orchestral Favorites'*, he turned in yet another stunningly good album with *'Joe's Garage'*.

This album has such a tight internal construction that it makes even *'Sheik Yerbouti'* seem disorganised, for in the steamy musical labyrinth of *'Joe's Garage'* the slightest sound or word is important and has a bearing on the story. Everything is intentional, and the numbers of musical cross references and reworkings are almost too numerous to list, making it appear as a musical encyclopaedia of the last twenty years. There is film, disco, glitter, rock, new-wave, country, rhythm and blues, plus snatches of Duane Eddy guitar, *'Sgt. Pepper'* saxophones and dabs of surf 'n' soda pop. Is that Mick and David strutting and fretting?

This is Joe's Garage band and their dreams. The whole 'stupid' story is introduced by the Central Scrutiniser, a sinister robotic humanoid, who explains that music must be made illegal and tells the story of Joe, Larry the future roadie, Mrs. Borg who wants to keep her son locked in the toilet, the Irish priest Father O'Riley, and Mary, an apprentice groupie. *'The Central Scrutiniser'* theme gives way to Stonesy harmonica-and-chewing-gum blues and surprises keep coming, as in *'Catholic Girls'* where Zappa swerves off 1960s vocalizing to tip his hat to Ruben Sano, a sixty-four-year-old crooner.

'Crew Slut' is a sleaze anthem telling of Dale Bozzio's perverse yearnings for leather groups. In *'Why Does It Hurt When I Pee?'* FM rock is taken to task after Joe discovers his lifestyle has given him 'an unpronounceable disease'. Finally he complains that *'Lucille Has Messed My Mind Up'* over a weepy pop ballad which had already appeared on a 'Jeff Simmons' album in 1969.

This is a very important album, part one of the serial. The question was, where would this excessiveness, which often appeared to be genius, lead?

Arthur Barrow, Ike Willis, Ray White, Bob Harris, F.Z, Tommy Mars, Vince Coliauta, Steve Vai.

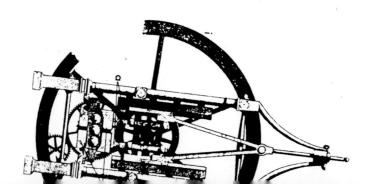

Joe's Garage, Acts 2 and 3

Zappa was off to a flying start with his new record company, and 'Sheik Yerbouti' went gold despite the deliberate confusion after Warners released what material they retained at the same time. 'Joe's Garage', which appeared a few months later, showed him on peak form.

The second Act shows Zappa at his most obsessed. Already in the first Act the hero Joe's mind and body had been played around with by girls, catholic or otherwise, to the extent of giving him his 'unpronounceable disease'. Act 2 contains surrealistic sexual symbolism a-go-go, classified X-rated obscenity at every line…stockings fetishes, necrophilia, felatio, cunnilingus, homosexual relationships with robots, transvestites, sado-masochism, inflatable rubber dolls and vibrators. The overall intent is to create the most over-the-top story line with pop stars, managers, groupies, de-frocked clerics, possessive mothers and rock critics. In the storyline music and sex have now been made illegal, and Joe joins the First Church of Appliantology, where he dresses up as a house-wife and has sex with a robot covered in marital aids. Having broken it, due to too much enthusiasm, he is sentenced to a jail sentence by the Central Scrutiniser, whose comments punctuate this incredible story. Here he meets an all-male cast of other 'criminals from the music business' and they spend their time 'snorting detergent and plooking each other".

There is a musical evolution in Act 2. Gone are the Sgt. Pepper-isms and 1960's guitar licks, and in come influences from black music: rhythm and blues, funk, spirituals and soul ballads. 'Stick It Out' is sung in German with Vocoder and is a neat combination of disco power-pop and doo-wop. 'Sy Borg' is based on jazz-rock synthesizer and has touches of Johnny Guitar Watson and Al Jarreau. Black gospel rears its head in 'Dong Work For Yuda', and a funky Keep It Greasy' rounds off Act 2.

Despite some catchy vocal parts Act 3 is mostly instrumental, a sort of hymn to the guitar. Joe is released from prison and still believes that 'music is the best' in 'Packard Goose'. Zappa immediately proves this in Water Melon In Easter Hay'. This must be his most majestic solo ever, full of emotional intensity and great sadness as Joe is forced to abandon music and take a conveyor-belt job, which gives rise to 'A Little Green Rosetta', a joke on industrial absurdity. 'Joe's Garage 1-3',is Zappa's concluding testament for the

1970s in the same manner that 'We're Only In It For The Money' concluded the 1960s.

Tinseltown Rebellion, 1981

'Tinseltown' is the sort of album that could be expected from an artist who over the course of almost thirty records has reached a sort of universality, and this varied audience is living proof of this. Frank Zappa constructs his own world which delights some and exasperates others. He has huge musical resources and tricks of his own invention, and he uses constant reworkings and cross references to his previous material, thus retaining the internal coherence for which Zappa is noted.

This well recorded live album, far from being a filler, captures the excitement of the concerts and also contains previously unreleased work. Many of the songs on 'Tinseltown' date from 1978; 'Easy Meat' and 'Bamboozled By Love' were not played in Europe until 1980.

The titles are taken from two different tours. Most of the album was recorded at Berkeley on the late '80 U.S. tour, and side four comes from London, 1979. 'Fine Girl' is a parody of FM rock, and snipes at the radio stations who have censured his work. It is immediately followed by 'Easy Meat', one of Zappa's best live pieces in recent years. Younger fans were pleased by the choice selection of very early material, 'Brown Shoes Don't Make It' and 'I Ain't Got No Heart' (1966) and 'Love Of My Life' (1962).

This is Zappa's first live career retrospective ('Mother Mania' was a studio selection) and is an excellent panorama of his live performances. It is far from disorganised, and lyrics and themes from one song often point the way to the next. Tinseltown is in part constructed from the two special booklets from the 80's tours.

Zappa also shows his indefatigable flair for acerbic irony, social comment and lyrical derision. In many ways 'Tinseltown' marks a welcome return to the humorously satirical verve of the past. There is a timely send up of oh-so-revolutionary Californian New Wave Punkery on the title track ('Tinseltown = Hollywood'). The album also contains breath of scandal as Zappa encourages the audience to throw their underpants and knickers up on stage ('Panty Rap'). These have now been turned into a kilt and hung in an American art gallery by their 'creator' Emily James.

'Tinseltown' is a good round up of Zappa's showmanship and also contains a tribute to one of his influences, Conlon Nancarrow ('Peaches III'). It is an eclectic and, for the new fans, educational album which strengthened Zappa's reputation as one of rock's most original and controversial father figures.

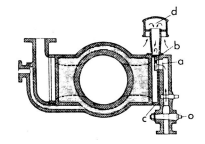

You Are What You Is, 1981

Most of the tracks here were played on the Fall Tour 1980, and were to become part of the set *'Crush All Boxes'*. Unlike *'Sheik Yerbouti'*, it is the vocal parts on *'You Are What You Is'* that grab the attention at first, although the musical arrangements are tight, snappy and concise yet extremely rich. Musically many of these songs could almost be radio-playlist hits but Zappa insists, of course, on sticking to his lyrical guns which are often socially subversive, philosophical or bizarrely obscure. At a time when many other bands were insipidly commercial, Zappa continued to construct his own universe of luxuriant fantasmagoria that was bursting with new ideas. This attitude effectively cut him off from wider exposure in the media, and the doors of radio and TV networks remained closed to such an independent freebooter, which must be why *'You Are...'* produced no hits, although it is Zappa's most thorough-going commercial effort to date.

The music is crisply effective and the subtle twists and turns of the vocal parts are virtuoso. Each song is linked to those before and after, and they reflect and justify each other in a variety of ways, which often gives the album the feel of a logical puzzle. If *'Absolutely Free'* was a modern rock oratorio, *'200 Motels'* was surrealist documentary and *'Joe's Garage'* was rock-opera, what is *'You Are What You Is'*? The panorama of 1980s America and its new beliefs – now Carter has gone and Reagan has come – passes under Zappa's expert microscope and emerges as a constantly changing visual symphony or film soundtrack with such a high degree of complexity and internal coherence that it can be listened to thousands of times without becoming boring, as Lao Tzeu would say.

Shut Up And Play Yer Guitar, 1981

The idea of distributing his records by mail order occurred to Zappa around 1969. Twelve years later he established this type of marketing system in America on his own Barking Pumpkin label with this three album boxed set which consists entirely of guitar solos. Before this the very idea of releasing a triple album of guitar solos would have made even the most open-minded record company A & R man roar with laughter or scream in terror. Such folk were obviously not ready for such a concept and were amazed at the immediate and continuing success of this album, which again demonstrates Zappa's sound knowledge of his public. The set won numerous awards in various countries, including the Grand Prix in France. Features on Zappa were run in various magazines and he started writing regular articles in 'Guitar Player'. Demand was so strong that the following year a 300 page book of his guitar solos came out.*

'Shut Up...' is a monument to the guitar and satisfied numerous fans who wanted to hear and re-hear solos played in concert. With one or two exceptions, the solos here are all live, and they move through a broad range of styles. There are crazily inspired improvisations, beautifully melodic pieces charged with emotion, tortured hard-rock howling, flurries of lightning-fast semi and demisemiquavers that resolve themselves in one long sustained note, and an extreme diversity of rhythmic accompaniment. This album amply demonstrates, in case anybody had not yet realized, that Zappa is a guitarist of the highest calibre, reaching pinnacles in rock playing comparable to Jeff Beck, Jimi Hendrix or Carlos Santana.

* See Zapparchives at end.

Ship Arriving Too Late To Save The Drowning Witch, 1982

An uninspiring album, barely saved by some well crafted pieces. There is a strange lack of direction and an unusual impression that much of it is filler material. Even keen Zappa fans found lump-fish hard to digest after acquiring a taste for caviar. Nevertheless he had a smash hit with 'Valley Girl', sung by his daughter, which surprised many people, and maybe even Zappa himself. Side two is the most substantial with 'Drowning Witch', and a long piece influenced by Conlon Nancarrow ('Envelopes').

The Man From Utopia, 1983

'The Man From Utopia' shows a new aspect of Zappa's music, the Sprech-Gesang, a mixture of speech and song in a rock context over bass glissandos and drum rolls. It also features his old friend Roy Estrada who contributes some unorthodox vocal parts. It is fine to experiment, but better to succeed, and two tracks, 'The Radio Is Broken' and 'The Dangerous Kitchen' don't really come off. This is a great shame as other songs sparkle in their apparent simplicity ('Mary Lou') or are superbly virtuoso ('Jazz Discharge Party Hats').

A rather lopsided album which, although it shows Zappa's restless intelligence heading in new directions, gives the impression of preaching to the converted. It is hard to imagine him recruiting many new followers with 'Drowning Witch' and 'Man From Utopia', despite their excellent sleeves by Roger Price and Tonino Liberatore.

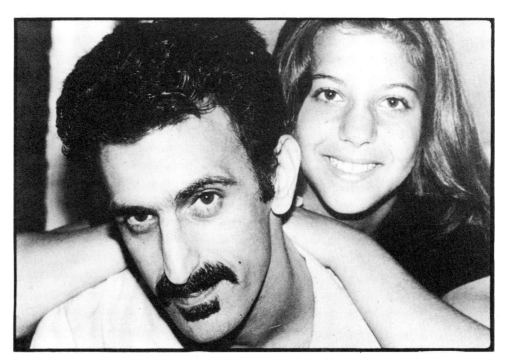

F.Z. And His Daughter Moon Unit.

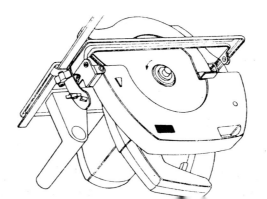

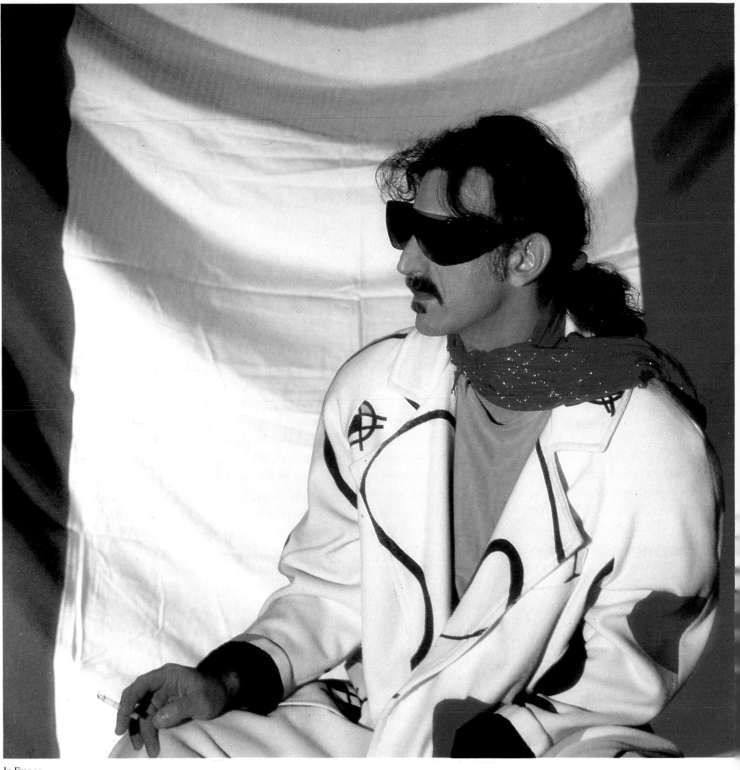

In France.

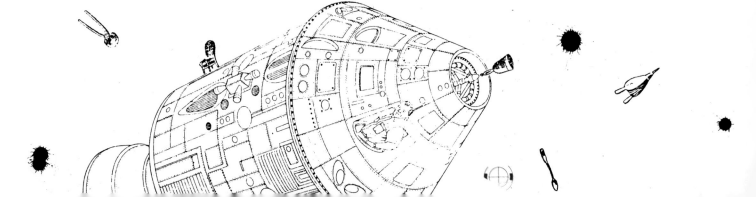

Soundtrack To Baby Snakes, 1983

This picture disc may seem less than fascinating at a casual glance since the track listing offers only one previously unrecorded song. But on listening to the record it becomes clear that this is an irreplaceable souvenir because of the quality of the playing and recording. Although the film aspect is, of course, lacking the heated, raunchy atmosphere, full of communicative energy, makes it all worthwhile. Zappa released the film as a video cassette. Terry Bozzio is especially effective, and Roy Estrada and Adrian Belew act the clown. Zappa fulfils his role as ring-master in his own musical theatre with the competence that has become one of his trademarks.

The London Symphony Orchestra. Zappa Volume 1, 1983

This album is a real gem, long awaited by those for whom Zappa is more than just a rock musician. It is not his first orchestral effort, but it is certainly his most perfected use of symphonic forms. It was recorded around January 11, 1983, at the Barbican Theatre, London, and the orchestra was conducted by Kent Nogano.

This recording is the fruit of about twenty years of underground work. Back in the 1950s Zappa was attracted to modern orchestral music and he wrote scores for 'The World's Greatest Sinner' and 'Run Home Slow.' This 'conceptual continuity' runs through 'Freak Out' and 'Uncle Meat', with their electric chamber orchestras, '200 Motels', a largely orchestral opera about rock, to this symphony orchestra of one hundred and eleven musicians.

All the pieces here are magnificent. Opening with 'Sad Jane', originally part of the ballet 'Bob In Dacron', it explores huge territories of sound, creating landscapes like a musical film. This reading of 'Envelopes' is closer to Charles Ives than Nancarrow. 'Moe's Herb Vacation', which takes up the whole of side two, is a long, involved and entirely absorbing orchestral adventure featuring the clarinet. The recording and mix quality are stunning. It is odd that today Zappa seems to regret the most daring gesture of the whole thing: using multi-track and studio re-recording techniques that belong to rock to record a symphony orchestra. This, like the music here, has never been heard of before!

The Perfect Stranger, 1984

Although Zappa's meeting with Pierre Boulez should have been a great event, the concert in Paris on January 9, 1984, was something of an anti-climax, perhaps because Zappa, at the height of the rock world, and Boulez, at the height of the avant-garde classical world, had little in common apart from their great professionalism, which led to a sort of culture-shock. The musicians of the Ensemble Intercontemporian were perhaps unfamiliar with Zappa's jazz and rock influences, for their accentuations were surprisingly stiff and inflexible. There was also a lack of contact between the sound-crews, and the Paris technicians looked at Zappa's people with their Sony PCM 3324 portable studio as if they had come from another planet. The two composers never really hit it off and a short time before the concert Boulez refused to comment on his partner, telling the newspaper Liberation:"'I reserve judgement about all the qualities of Zappa's music'."

It is perhaps because of this that the album is not as successful as the 'Symphony Orchestra' work, especially 'Dupree's Paradise' a piece which was clearly 'too American' for the Old Continent's classical specialists. The orchestra's meticulous interpretation of the 'The Perfect Stranger' (the track) is also impressive, but the best pieces on here are the ones where Zappa experiments with his new musical computer, the synclavier. In these electronic compositions he uses new sounds that contemporary classical composers have not yet tried. They are dissonant, atonal pieces which still have melodies and rhythms.

Them Or Us, 1984

After the disappointments of 'Drowning Witch' and 'Man From Utopia', Zappa released a good, guitar based rock album, complete with an excellent sleeve design by Donald Roller Watson that featured the dog Patricia who also appears on the cover of 'The Perfect Stranger'. Production is of the very high standard that people have come to expect from Zappa, and his talents as sound engineer and arranger are as much in evidence as his qualities as composer, songwriter and guitarist.

'Them Or Us' is very varied, with impressive use of backwards tape in 'Ya Hozna'. 'The Closer You Are' is built on shimmering harmonies, 'In France' is chunky blues, 'Stevies' Spanking' is raucous rock, but whatever the style adopted, the harmonic detail is striking, even on a jokey little song like 'Baby Take Your Teeth Out' whose middle section appears to be inspired by Mingus' 'Passions Of A Man' (from the record 'Oh Yeah'). 'Be In My Video' is a humorous dig at David Bowie type videoisms: 'Let's try to look sincere/While we dance the blues/Under the megawatt moonlight/Pretend to be Chinese'. 'Them Or Us' has some old faces, George Duke, Johnny Guitar Watson and Napoleon Murphy Brock, but none appear on this double LP's best track, 'Sinister Footwear II', an instrumental. 'Them Or Us' is a round-up of numerous styles and ideas, and probably contains something for everyone, even Boy George!

Thingfish, 1984

This is a three album set of musical comedy (for details, see Zapparchives). Few will have the patience to listen right through. Zappa had part of it published with photos in Hustler Magazine, but this is not the only controversial factor in this anthology of trendy America's hang-ups for the hard-core Zappa-ist. It must be his most uncommercial album ever. Most of the text is in a sort of Broadway Sprech-Gesang (spoken song). As if this was not enough, Zappa's incredible slang-parodies and inventive use of language makes it absolutely necessary to read the libretto. This is Zappa at his most arrogantly radical. It is doubtful whether 'Thingfish' could be performed on stage, and may well exasperate as many as it delights, but it is a chilling picture of a world sliding towards THEM or US!

Old Masters, 1985

In the history of rock, *'Freak Out'* will be remembered as the first concept album, *'Absolutely Free'* as the first collage album, *'Lumpy Gravy'* as the first piece of fully symphonic rock, *'We're Only In It For The Money'* as the first socio-satirical commentary and *'Ruben And The Jets'* as the first nostalgia disc.

Zappa is a force of musical 'thought in motion'. He has never been static, and whatever his distribution set-up has never stopped perfecting musical strategies. He has been stealthily creeping up on an astonishingly wide range of music, catching it and setting it down. The tactics for the next album depends on the resounding success or relative failure of the previous one. By balancing provocation and refinement, intelligence and clownishness, he has strategically dodged the pitfalls of pandering to his enemies (show-biz and radio predominantly) and gone far beyond to open up whole new areas of music and ideas while always remaining open to new opportunities.

But before all this there were the lean times: aborted projects, small jobs, studio hassles, seedy bars. This is captured on the *'Mystery Disc'*, which starts with the superb theme from *'Run Home Slow'*, followed by the equally good *'Duke Of Prunes'* from the same film. There is also a sound collage recorded the evening Zappa opened Studio Z on which you can hear early sound experiments, many of which resurface in later works. Jim Sherwood and Ray Collins are already present, as is Don Van Vliet, who was making a little sci-fi film with his friend Zappa called *'Captain Beefheart Versus The Grunt People.'* It was from this never finished project that the Captain adopted his stage name. During this period (1963-4) Zappa was performing in places like the Village Inn at Sun Village.

The only complaint is that Zappa did not see fit to include *'Ned The Mumbler'* and *'Ned Has A Brainstorm'* with *'I Was A Teenage Malt Shop'*, which was also to be the first rock opera in 1963.

The *'Old Masters'* themselves only returned to their creator's possession after a long and costly lawsuit with two record companies, a manager and his lawyer brother. When Zappa retrieved them they were in a terrible state as they had been stored in bad conditions. Some, like *'We're Only In It For The Money'*, were almost transparent. Before digitally remastering the whole lot, Zappa had to spend almost three

months performing plastic surgery until he was able to offer quality worthy of the most modern recording techniques. The result is fantastic, even though bits of *'Ruben And The Jets'* and *'We're Only…'* had to be remixed. The old masters are an absolute must for any self-respecting Zappa nut.

Frank Zappa Meets The Mothers Of Prevention, 1985

Zappa is no stranger to censorship. Back in the 1960s Verve removed lyrics they found shocking, there was the *'Punky's Whips'* fiasco with Warners, and Mercury were upset by *'I Don't Wanna Get Drafted'*, which finally came out on Columbia. More recently his new distributor MCA refused to handle *'Thingfish'* after the outrage of 'a little lady at the control room plant', and a born-again printer who refused to work on the libretto text. Exit Zappa to Capitol where, to be on the safe side, he had a *'Warning/Guarantee'* sticker put on the box, which said that the work contained 'material which a truly free society would neither fear nor suppress'. It also attacked some 'socially retarded areas, religious fanatics and ultra-conservative political organisations' who 'violate the first Amendment rights by attempting to censor rock and roll albums'.

He was thus well prepared in 1985 when an influential hysteria group organized a campaign in the U.S. under the name 'The Parent's Music Resource Centre'. An official list of its members was never disclosed, but it appeared to consist mainly of women whose shared characteristic was that their husbands were influential politicians in Congress and the Senate Commerce Committee. On September 19 the 'Washington Wives' and other merchants in 'Fundamentalist Frogwash' (as they were nicknamed) decided to ban any references to 'sex, violence, drugs and satanism' in rock lyrics, and singled out Prince, Madonna, WASP and AC/DC as particularly offensive. They demanded that X-rated stickers should be made compulsory for such artists.

This sparked off a much publicised media battle in which Zappa took an active part. He went in for a real audio-visual marathon, going from local radio to national television, frequently appearing on the big networks ABC and CBS at all times of day, defending his case with such calm articulacy that the 'Washington Wives' were unwilling to confront him on the air, and only attacked him second hand, as if afraid to look ridiculous.

There is insufficient space here to go into the details of an affair which caused such

an uproar that *Rolling Stone, People* magazine and most TV networks covered it fully. It ended at the Senate Commerce Committee on September 19, and it is clear that even if this horrendous effort at censorship has been overcome (or if it is applied, it will certainly have to be more subtle), it has at least allowed the world to learn about the sexual frustrations of American politician's wives, and their total ignorance of the problems, both sexual and otherwise, facing young people in America and elsewhere.

If you have not read Zappa's open letter to the music industry on the subject, or his dossier on it, or seen the articles in the American and international press, the masterpiece from this album, *'Porn Wars'*, will fill you in. It is a fascinating collage made up from the voices of the senators and their wives accelerated, slowed, overdubbed at all sorts of speeds, against a background of computer music, combined with extracts from oldies like *'Lumpy Gravy'* with a *'Thingfish'* style dialogue. Although using infinitely better equipment these days, this piece is a reminder of the fact that Zappa was a good twenty years ahead of his time on *'We're Only In It For The Money'*, and this is a similar synthesis of social commentary and sound collage. On *'Porn Wars'* Zappa reminds those who only appreciated the provocative face of the 1960s that his modernity already lay in his composition techniques. It is ultimately pointless to regret the crazy wind that blew through the decade, like some nostalgic freaks, for even if Zappa's music may seem at first glance more technically accomplished and less crazy today, it is this constant search for new sounds, techniques of composition, and instruments which make him seem so crazily modernistic.

This album contains two examples of Zappa's new preoccupations: *'Little Beige Sambo'* is a piece influenced by Nancarrow, and *'Aerobics In Bondage'* is a sort of electronic concerto in which no human being took part. It is totally 'untouched by human hands'. For those who may find this disconcerting, the other side opens with the more mainstream *'We're Turning Again'* (about fans of Jim, Janis, Donovan etc) followed by the instrumental *'Alien Orifice'* which also dates from 1981 and a little dig at jazzy, top-ranking session musicians from the Berklee School called 'Yo Cats'. *'What's New In Baltimore'* rounds the album off beautifully with a grandiose guitar solo.

Does Humor Belong In Music? 1986

Among Zappa's numerous experiments there is one he calls *'Xenocrony'* or *'Strange Synchronization'*. This is technically complex in practice but simple in theory: parts of different songs (guitar solos, drums, etc) are remodelled and synchronized to form a new piece of music. The first fruits of this concept were on *'Joe's Garage'* in a live context (*'Sheik Yerbouti'*). Throughout Zappa's work themes have the potential to be reworked to form the basis of new themes on a new album, but the extremist quality of FZ's music pushes this logic to its limits. It moves from handwritten scores to a collage made up of previously prepared sections which are also meticulously composed. Solos experimented with in concert are used as a basis for studio composition and vice-versa. In fact, it is impossible in the final result to know which is live and which is studio. On *'Does Humor..'* Zappa has taken the joke even further. In the sleeve notes he says 'no overdubs'. Sure Frank, there may be no overdubs, but there's plenty of montage. Most of the tracks here are composed of numerous parts, one of which may come from London, one from Chicago and one from Los Angeles. The ultimate refinement in Xenocrony.

All the material here is 100% live, and totally digital. It is one hour of brilliant music on compact disc. All the solos, especially on *'Zoot Allures'*, *'What's New In Baltimore'* and *'Let's Move To Cleveland'* are marvellous, a guaranteed aural treat, and *'Does Humor…'* is an excellent live panorama, made up of a variety of ingredients from the 'wine, port and pepper of *'Let's Move…'* Dweezil (Zappa junior) keeps up the family tradition by playing an increasingly important role in the music, particularly on *'Whippin' Post'*. Alan Zovod's very *'Little House'* (*'Burnt Weeny'*) solo spiced with *'Eat That Question'* (*'Grand Wazoo'*) is also noteworthy.

'Does Humor Belong In Music' formally gives lie to those imbecile journalists who still insist that Zappa has peaked, and also heralds new adventures in sight and sound.

6

THE ORACLE HAS IT ALL PSYCHED OUT

AND OTHER ARTICLES

BY ZAPPA

Frank V. Zappa Sr, F.Z, Bob, Mrs Zappa, Carl, Candy.

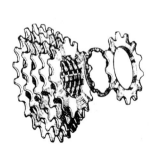

'50s Teenagers And '50s Rock

All teenagers are fad-conscious and follow the leader. Because of this, a certain ideal image will usually come to pervade an entire school. During the '50s, I went to four separate high schools. Although each was in Southern California, their images were distinctly different. I went, in chronological order, to Claremont, Grossmont High School in El Cajon near San Diego, Mission Bay High School in San Diego, and Antelope Valley High School in Lancaster, where I graduated.

Claremont's nice. It's green. It's got little old ladies running around in electric karts. The kids are all reserved, want to graduate from high school, and go to colleges around the corner. When I went there, they were preparing for this by dressing California Ivy or Buckle Back A Go Go.

At Grossmont High School, the only things the kids had to be proud of were the size of their student body and the fact that their marching band was really spiffy. Grossmont didn't have just middle and upper middle-class whites, but those it did dressed Buckle Back, though not as severely as Claremont. They wanted to go to San Diego State 'cause they thought it was swinging, or Tempe, in Arizona, 'cause they had heard it was a party school. Their image was superficially clean. They didn't come to class drunk out of their minds: they saved boozing for the weekend. Mission Bay was different.

First, it was a very transient neighborhood; a lot of the kids' fathers worked in the navy. It was definitely juvenile delinquent territory. You wore a leather jacket and very very greasy hair. You carried a knife and chain. If you were really bad, you mounted razor blades in the edge of your shoes for kicking. Also, you made sure you carved up the school's linoleum floor by wearing taps on your soles. If you failed to do any of these things you would (1) not get any sex action and (2) probably be injured.

And, like *Blackboard Jungle*, teachers weren't safe either. In fact, there was a big scandal in San Diego when I was at Mission Bay, because at San Diego High, the teachers were being threatened by knives and other weapons if they wouldn't give the kids money on request. A kid would come up to a teacher in the halls and say, 'Gimme a dime, man'. If the teacher didn't deliver, he was beat up. A while after all this, the newspapers released a story alleging that the police had sent in undercover agents to spy on the kids, and that these agents had gathered all sorts of information. This got the kids very pissed off, and, in retaliation, the violence increased. Kids were proud of the violence in their schools. They didn't want to have some ninny school. They wanted a rough school.

Any figure who was alienated became a potential idol. This could take strange turns. There was a lot of identification with James Dean, but there was also a lot of identification with *'I Was A Teenage Werewolf'*. In that movie, an evil doctor turns a teenager into a werewolf. Naturally, the teenager is alienated, and the doctor, being an adult, is someone to blame. This stuff is going on all the time. Madison Avenue is constantly injecting people with product desires which turn them into mad consumers. The people I hung around with were sold on monsters and horror of every kind. And if I sat down to draw a picture, you could bet it would be a monster. It was great to laugh at that stuff – that's why we loved it – so we could convince ourselves it didn't scare us, that something didn't scare us. I couldn't stand any other type of movie. I saw stuff like *'Wasp Woman'*. The *'Beast Of Haunted Cave'*, and (very good!) *'Attack Of The Killer Shrews'*.

In *'Not Of This Earth'*, a dude wearing wraparound glasses takes this thing out of a tube. It looks like a stretched piece of wizened romaine lettuce. He sets it on a table and right away it starts puffing up. Then it picks up and hovers off through the window until it comes in some other guy's window. It drifts over to the guy, hovers above him, then drops – woosh – around his head, and, closing in, bites him. It's great! The blood is coming from underneath onto his white shirt and he's going "Whhaaarrghh!". I saw that three times and when I had learned to tell just when that thing was going to get him, I'd sit behind some noisy kids, and right at the exact second, grab the kid's throat, and then, in a flash, sit right back. Panic out!

Out of a town's neighborhood theaters, there would be one where all the teenagers went. It was comparable to a '50s Fillmore, or any of your local psychedelic dungeons of today. Nobody really cared what was being shown. It was just a dark place where guys went to meet some girl who they tried to make it with later, if not there. There was this one theater in Lancaster where, looking down the seats, you'd see a bead here, another one there, fine, but then you'd see some huddled lump of blankets or clothes that was moving, and then another and another. And then you'd notice all these bodies jammed in weird positions against the walls – Kama Sutra 375 with a leg sticking up – and the monster was happening on the screen. It was really great!

My fascination with monsters extended, like that of a lot of other kids, to comics. Horror comics. All the things EC did – *The Vault Of Horror, Tales From The Crypt,* that stuff. *Mad* was big too, appealing as it did to a certain lunatic fringe with a certain type of humor. Those were comics that girls used to glance at and go, 'Eeeewe!'. And some of that stuff was a little raunchy. I remember reading a *'Plastic Man'* comic where a guy blew his nose on his coat tail with the word snork above it. Heavy business for the children in those days.

By the time I was really into high school, however, comics were fairly puny and stayed that way for me until Marvel came out. I read them now. And I'd only go to the movies maybe twice a month. My real social life revolved around records and the band I played with. There wasn't much work for us then. We'd get a job maybe, every two months at a teen hop, but most of the time, I was back in my room listening to records. It was the records, not TV, which I didn't watch, that brainwashed me. I'd listen to them over and over again. The ones I couldn't buy. I'd steal, and the ones I couldn't steal I'd borrow, but I'd get them somehow. I had about six hundred records – 45s – at one time, and I swear I knew the title, group and label of every one. We all used to quiz each other. We really liked records that featured guitars. If you remember, the featured instrument in early rock was the saxophone. It was very phallic. This guy, Joe Houston used to do a number where he'd wind up bending over backwards just squawking out this one raucous note. Now that the guitar is the predominant instrument, it has been redesigned to look less feminine and more phallic – flatter, with long skinnier necks. The visual part of music, the actual playing, is seeing very interesting developments.

And though every gang hated what is now known as the Establishment, each had their own style, and hated any other gang almost as much. Each top gang of the school hated the neighboring schools' top gang; hated their guts. The gangs with the cycle boots never did get along with the gang with the peggers and French-toed shoes, khakis and Sir Guy shirts. The Mexicans hated the Negroes. The Negroes hated the Mexicans. They both hated the whites who hated them back.

On one famous occasion, several gangs from Watts, who had temporarily joined forces, came down in an autocade to wipe out an area in San Diego known as Logan Heights. Logan Heights rallied in an all-out concerted effort and beat the crap out of them. It didn't even make the school paper, but the kids all knew. It was their victory.

My parents didn't let me have a car (I didn't get one until I was twenty-three years old), and nobody would take me riding with them because I was unpopular. So I missed out on the real monstro-fights. But I was involved in some locker room rumbles, so I have a pretty good idea of what that punch-out mystique is all about.

Of course, now, most of those feelings have been sublimated into zapem-with-love which hides a lot of hostility. Deep down they know it's a lie. They can't believe all that flower power wonderment because they can't make it work. Drugs are largely responsible for this sublimation – they get too stoned to have any sex energy, let alone fight, which was the substitute for sex in the first place. This transition is evident in current pop music lyrics where sensations associated with the consumption of certain types of chemicals have blended with, been confused with, distorted, and, at times, completely replace the sex/love sensations/emotions of years back. Bushes and flashes instead of feeling and reeling, diamonds and rubies instead of empty arms and broken hearts.

I've played dances and even lectured at a couple of high schools, and those kids are really into a drug culture, a drug mystique. They've got a whole new set of fads. Leather arm bands, beads, feathers, weird clothes, and long hair are the L.D. bracelets, madras shirts, Princeton haircuts and loafers with pennies in them of today. No matter what they wear, the bulk of kids in the U.S. continue to think as their parents do, adopting the old prejudices and stupidities in a different disguise and repackaging them in their own level. Sure, there have been some real basic changes in the attitudes of some kids, but not nearly enough.

A lot of things look like they've changed more than they really have. For instance, all this dropping out. Today if a kid splits from his home and lives in the streets, he can always join up with some hippies – some group that will take him in. In the '50s, no one dropped out. You left the house and you were an adult and had to go punch it out with all of them. The main reason a kid would be in the streets then was to participate in a gang fight. It's easy to overestimate kids' independence from the family when they've just exchanged them.

The underground gets a lot of press coverage today: it didn't get much at all in the '50s. Elvis Presley was the most widely known figure, and, in my group he was liked mostly by the girls and younger guys. But in San Diego, which is a good town for blues, a lot of the boys liked Howlin' Wolf and B.B. King better. Their music was stronger and the kids responded to it. Also, blues is usually appreciated most by people who feel themselves alienated and oppressed, regardless of education or economics. The blues lovers I knew then, the ones with the leather jackets, certainly were those kind of people. They felt oppressed by everything, and they were the ones who developed all that teenage slang. It never came from the madras shirt set who only took over and adopted some collegiate expressions, probably from their older brothers and sisters. The real gritty slang came from those guys who felt themselves so threatened that they would do everything they could to look hard even if they didn't get a chance to act hard. And the reason it developed is very similar to the reason slaves in the South developed their own talk – to fool their masters, to make them feel superior, exclusive. Same thing with the clothing and hair styles. Some of these guys from that period are still around. In East L.A. guys in their early thirties who still wear DA's and peggers are called veteranos. In fact, most of the gangs I was familiar with were Mexican, and a lot of those guys – the Pachucos – still dress and think the same way today. Most of them married their old girl friends and are working in a garage.

As for our taste in singers, my set just wouldn't listen to any white rock. It was always punier than the black stuff, and a lot of it was simply inept imitation. But then I was lucky to have black rock available, since the musical taste of a community not only affects, but is, in turn, affected by what is available at the moment. For instance, Claremont just had Dixie and semi-classical in its main record store. Many people hadn't even heard of someone like Muddy Waters. The blues freak of the '50s was a real rarity.

So, a statement that appeared in some newspaper article about pop music, saying how great it is that we have finally gotten away from the puerile slush of the '50s, was probably made by someone who never heard any of that decade's great R&B numbers. He probably only heard stuff on easy access labels like Liberty, Dot and maybe Capitol. And, even if you were into R&B at that time, there was still another strata, one beneath the R&B records. If you knew and liked R&B, then you knew Little Willie John and Hank Ballard on the King label. Once you found a store, they were as easy to get as Pat Boone on Dot was for all America. But some of the best really happening stuff was strictly oneshot. It would be a monumental job of research to list all the little label releases during that time. Companies were being formed everywhere. For instance, in Arizona there was a company that put out Bat Records. Maybe they put out only one record, maybe hundreds. It was so small, you don't know. For records like that, you really had to scuttle around, haunt places that sold used jukebox records from the South. If you did that kind of scouting, you might come across someone like Roy Tan.

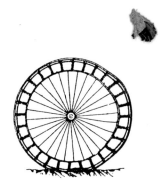

In 1956, I hit upon the only record of this Roy Tan I ever saw. It was called *'I Don't Like It',* and it was on the Tan label. Hmmmn, it went like this:

You been rockin on my baby.
And I don't like it.
I'm warnin' you daddy-o
I'll hammer your head so low
You'll look mighty funny you must admit
Unbuttoning your collar to talk a bit.
So quit rockin' on my baby. I don't like it,
Daddy, you got to go.

The other side starts like this: Roy Tan: *"Ah, you tend to spring chicken. Girl, what's your name?"* Girl: *"My name's Isabella and I'm off to a party. I can't talk to you right now."* Then Roy breaks into song:

Isabella, Isabella,
Won't you tell me where the party's gonna be?
Don't treat me like a stranger
And leave me like the Ranger
All alone.
I've got a dollar in my pocket
And I want to rock it
Can't you see?

Oh, man, they were really talking some good stuff then. Compare that with tutti frutti, awroottie by the time Pat Boone got through with it, and the whole thing's ridiculous.

Another great label, besides Tan, was Dootone, the one that first released *'Earth Angel',* by the Penguins, but they had a lot of other great stuff like *'Love Will Make Your Mind Go Wild',* which had to dance on the other side – *'The Ookey Ook.'* Then there was *'Ay Si Si She Likes to Mambo',* which had the odd line about how radios were turned low down so nobody could see 'em when they really went to town. As if the radio was controlling the lights in the room.

One of the strangest, if not *the* strangest record of all time wasn't a one-shot, but came out on the other side of *'Teardrops'* by Lee Andrews and the Hearts. *'Teardrops',* a love song, was the big hit and *'The Girl Around The Corner'* was passed over, but it's fantastic. It's the most abstract lyric I've ever heard – highly stylized. It has to do with a girl named Buddha Macrae and a guy named Butchie Stover who 'makes love like a Casanova'. This guy is telling about some chick around the corner and how far out she is, and he succeeds, while all the time, someone in the background is going *'Bum Bum Dee-Bahcha'*. I still can't figure it out, it's insane. And if I ever met this Buddha Macrae chick, I'd uh…I don't think I could handle it.

I have a few friends who come over to the house, and we whip through those 45s of mine three to four times a month 'til they're coming out of our ears. It's like a time machine; takes me right back to school days. I can almost smell what was cooking in the kitchen when I first heard them. And in the Ruben And The Jets album, I very consciously took all those hot numbers – *'Nite Owl'* and *'Cherry Pie'* – all of them, and blended them in combinations to come up with my songs. I even mixed parts of the *'The Rite Of Spring'* with the Moonglow's style of harmony. I took some of their better lines too.

Love lyrics were some of the best things in the old R&B. If you listened to the words superficially, you might have thought they were talking about 'old love' – hold hands, kiss her, ask her out – but they weren't. They were talking about getting laid. The beginning of the sexual revolution is chronicled in song and story on those oldies. Also, if you took all those songs with the ice-cream cone changes, (there must have been thousands):

DAA DA-DA-DA
DAA DA-DA-DA
DAA DA-DA-DA
DAA

and pumped them all into a computer, you would come out with a very exact social moral code for the kids of that day. It's the best history you could get because it's all in there: prejudices, beliefs, disbeliefs, social practices – everything.

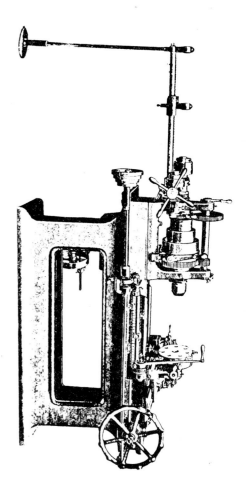

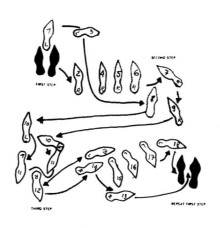

LISTENING TO THE NIFTY BEAT OF RUBEN & THE JETS WILL UNDOUBTEDLY MAKE YOU WANT TO DO THE BOP. THE URGE TO DANCE WILL OVERPOWER YOU. BECAUSE OF THIS UNCONTROLABLE FORCE, A PAGE OF DETAILED BOP DANCE STEP INSTRUCTIONS IS ENCLOSED

Looking at the main attraction of that time, Elvis Presley, and the superstars of now, The Beatles, some interesting changes seem to have taken place in terms of how an audience chooses its idol. I think Ralph Gleason is right when he calls The Beatles an ideal projection of the audience's personalities, and Presley a strictly sexual phenomenon. Presley, when he first hit, did not have a new image. He already existed in the masses and was easy to identify with. But The Beatles created a wholly new image that was foreign, no pun, to America. Presley's impact, the way he moved and sang, was so sexual that he was too much of a threat to the teenyboppers of those days, and eventually had to sing songs that reversed the sexual roles, making him the passive in such tunes as 'Love Me Tender' or 'Any Way You Want Me To Be'. So along come The Beatles, who look so cute and harmless that they are allowed to sing dominant songs. Their sexual innuendo was verbal and subtle and they got away with it.

Then long hair happened. In the early days of Beatlemania, a guy with long hair had about a three hundred percent better chance of getting laid than a guy without (the chick being so stupid as to automatically assume 'He's either an English pop star or he's in a group or *something*'). But whatever her fantasy, she was sure he was way cuter than the guy in the corner with the greasy mop. This dictating of fashion by chicks for men, this power, was a very important part of Beatlemania. So, if you were a madras-shirt man, you could safely grow your hair – a little bit – and become an ersatz Beatle and get laid. Then, when The Rolling Stones hit, and there were all those pictures of Bill Wyman with that real long, scraggly black hair, hippie packaging really began. Now if you had been a motorcycle fug you would grow your hair longer, wear even dirtier clothes, and get action without having to go mod and cute. You were provided with a fashion image too.

At one point during Beatlemania, the guys started faking English accents and really pulled the wool over the chick's eyes. Of course, after going that far, the next step was to get a band together just like The Beatles and have more glamor. 'Let's get in there and then we can play a job at the dance'. So they started learning how to play like Beatle records from scratch. Some got tired of imitating and, wholly by accident, started playing their own music. But most found it hard to break their imitative image even if they wanted to since there's always some schumcko beer bar owner who wants a

Beatle or a Rolling Stones band, and will pay for it. Even at fraternity drink-outs, if you don't sound like Jimi Hendrix or Eric Clapton, they don't even want you to play. The boys are just as narrow as the girls. Actually, some of the girls have improved. In fact, the main difference between then and now is that there are about ten percent less puny-minded girls. Consider for a girl to have status in the '50s, she had to wear her dress sticking out with all those starchy petticoats and eat her lunch on the school's front lawn and be a cheerleader. She had to be 'real cute' and sublimate sex feelings with school spirit, student government, church or whatever.

Today, for a girl to have status, she has to make it with a rock star. I find this to be a definite improvement.

(f209Evergreen 1970.

The Oracle Has It All; The New Rock By Frank Zappa.

Rock music is a necessary element of contemporary society. It is functional. It is healthy and valid artistically. It is also educational (how to ask a girl for a date, what love is like). It has all the answers to what your mother and father won't tell you. It is also a big business. This is a brief history of rock and its relationship to our society. TO TEE OFF. A nifty questionnaire to get you interested so you'll read the rest of the article:

Part One: The '50s.

1. Who remembers beer? White port and lemon juice? For 10 points, what was the name of the guy in your school who used to buy your juice for parties...

2. Who remembers making out and getting hot? For 10 points, how old were you when it happened...

3. Who remembers duck tails, peggers, leather jackets, bunny shoes, brogans, tight sweaters, teardrops, full skirts with a million starchy petticoats. Sir Gary shirts and khakis? For 10 points, how much did you pay for your St. Christopher medallion...

4. Who remembers gang fights, tire chains, boys with razor blades in the toes of their wedgies, girls with razor blades in their hair, blood and sickening crunch? For 10 points, tell why the cops were afraid of your gang...

Part Two: The '60s.

5. Who remembers speed? Smoke? Acid? Transcendental meditation? For 10 points, name your connection or guru...

6. Who remembers getting stoned and having an orgy? For 10 points, how old were you when you learned you were incapable of relating to others in a tender, personal way and finally discovered you had become asexual...

7. Who remembers electric hair, bell bottoms, plastic jackets, sandals, high boots, bulky knit sweaters, Guccis, miniskirts, De Voss shirts and velvet pants? For 10 points, look around the house, find your beads and bells and recite Hare Krishna without laughing...

8. Who remembers demonstrations, truncheons, Mace, police dogs, the Pentagon, Century City, blood and sickening crunch? For 10 points, tell why you were afraid to cut your hair, infiltrate the establishment, and do it the easy way...

Our present state of socio-sexual enlightenment is, to a certain extent, attributable to the evolution of rock and vice versa. Our story begins back in...the good old days, at the recreation centers, no Levis or capris please. 'School functions' and 'teen hops' were real swell and keen and acceptable to Mom and Dad. They were also dull unless you liked to dance a fox-trot as the high school swing band fumbled through an evening of Combo Orks and reprocessed Glenn Miller. The kids would be holding on to each other desperately and sweating. The chaperon would come along and say "Seven inches apart please," and hold a sawed-off ruler between you and the girl.

Society was very repressed, sexually, and dancing was a desperate attempt to get a little physical contact with the opposite sex. Free love, groupies, the Plaster Casters of Chicago and such bizarre variants, and the G.T.O.s of Laurel Canyon in L.A. didn't exist then. Preoccupation with sexual matters accounted for a disproportionate amount of the daily conscious thought process and diverted a lot of energy from schoolwork.

This and the low quality of teaching in many schools, caused kids to seek education in the streets. Youth gangs with marvellous names and frightening reputations cruised the streets at night, searching for ways to compensate for the lack of sexually approachable girls. Vandalism and assorted manglings became acceptable substitutes for 'teen-sex'. Young men would compete, like cowboy gunfighters, to be 'the baddest cat.' This dubious honor would generally entitle its bearer to boss the gang and in some instances, preferential treatment from those few daring girls who would go 'all the way'.

Parents, unfortunately, have a tendency to misunderstand, misinterpret, and, worst of all, ridicule patterns of behaviour which seem foreign to them. When they noticed a growing interest among teen-agers in matters pertaining to the pleasure-giving functions of the body, they felt threatened. Mom and Dad were sexually uninformed and inhibited (a lot of things wrong with society today are directly attributable to the fact that the people who make the laws are sexually maladjusted) and they saw no reason why their kids should be raised differently. Why should those dirty teen-agers have all the fun? Sex is for making babies and it makes your body misshapen and ugly afterward and let's not talk about it shall we?

The Big Note; Digression 1

In the Abnuceals Emuukha Electric Symphony Orchestra album *'Lumpy Gravy'* there is a section on side two where several unidentified characters discuss the origins of the universe. One of the characters explains the concept of the Big Note; everything in the universe is composed basically of vibrations – light is a vibration, sound is a vibration, atoms are composed of vibrations – and all these vibrations just might be harmonics of some incomprehensible fundamental cosmic tone.

How important is sound? I participated in a conversation recently with Herbie Cohen (our manager) about rumors of a government research project. The project, it seems, has been going on for several years. What does sound do to plants? According to Herbie, a field of corn increased its yield – the individual ears even got bigger – because the research team set up loudspeakers in the field and pumped in some music. According to Herbie, the next step is to find out what kind of music the vegetables like the best.

The ways in which sound affects the human organism are myriad and subtle. Why does the sound of Eric Clapton's guitar give one girl a sensation which she describes as 'Bone Conduction'? Would she still experience Bone Conduction if Eric, using the same extremely loud thick tone, played nothing but Hawaiian music? Which is more important: the timbre (color-texture) of a sound, the succession of intervals that make up melody, the harmonic support (chords) which tells your ear 'what the melody means' (is it major or minor or neutral or what), the volume at which the sound is heard, the volume at which the sound is produced, the distance from source to ear, the density of the sound, the number of sounds per second or fraction thereof…and so on? Which of these would be the most important element in an audial experience which gave you a pleasurable sensation? An erotic sensation? Look at kids in school, tapping their feet, beating with their fingers. People try unconsciously to be in tune with their environment. In a variety of ways, even the most 'unconcerned' people make attempts to 'tune up' with their God. Hal Zeiger (one of the first big promoters of rock entertainment during the 50s) says: "I knew that there was a big thing here that was basic, that was big, that had to get bigger. I realized that this music got through to the youngsters because the big beat matched the great rhythms of the human body. I understood that. I knew it and I knew there was nothing that anyone could do to knock that out of them. And I further knew that they would carry this with them the rest of their lives."

Rock Around The Clock

In my days of flaming youth I was extremely suspect of any rock music played by white people. The sincerity and emotional intensity of their performances, when they sang, about boyfriends and girl friends and breaking up etc., was nowhere when I compared it to my high school Negro R&B heroes like Johnny Otis, Howlin' Wolf and Willie Mae Thornton.

But then I remember going to see *Blackboard Jungle.* When the titles flashed up there on the screen Bill Haley and his Comets started blurching *'One Two Three O'Clock, Four O'Clock Rock…'* It was the loudest rock sound kids had ever heard at that time. I remember being inspired with awe. In cruddy little teen-age rooms, across America, kids had been huddling around old radios and cheap record players listening to the 'dirty music' of their life style. ("Go in your room if you wanna listen to that crap…and turn the volume all the way down".) But in the theater watching *Blackboard Jungle,* they couldn't tell you to turn it down. I didn't care if Bill Haley was white or sincere…he was playing the Teen-Age National Anthem and it was so LOUD I was jumping up and down. *Blackboard Jungle,* not even considering the story line which had the old people winning in the end represented a strange sort of 'endorsement' of the teen-age cause: 'They have made a movie about us, therefore, we exist…"

Responding like dogs, some of the kids began to go for the throat. Open rebellion. The early public dances and shows which featured rock were frowned upon by the respectable parents of the community. They did everything they could do to make it impossible for these events to take place. They did everything they could to shield their impressionable young ones from the ravages of this vulgar new craze. (Hal Zeiger: "They did everything they could to make sure their children were not moved erotically by Negroes.")

From the very beginning, the real reason Mr. & Mrs. Clean White America objected to this music was the fact that it was performed by Black people. There was always the danger that one night – maybe in the middle of the summer, in a little pink party dress – Janey or Suzy might be overwhelmed by the lewd, pulsating jungle rhythms and do something to make their parents ashamed.

Parents, in trying to protect their offspring from whatever danger they imagined to be lurking within the secret compartments of this new musical vehicle, actually helped to shove them in front of it whereupon they were immediately run over. The attitude of parents helped to create a climate wherein the usage of rock music (as a pacifier or perhaps anaesthetic experience) became very necessary. Parents offered nothing to their children that could match the appeal of rock. It was obvious to the kids that anyone who did not like (or at least attempt to understand) rock music, had a warped sense of values. To deny rock music its place in the society was to deny sexuality. Any parent who tried to keep his child from listening to or participating in this musical ritual was, in the eyes of the child, trying to castrate him.

There was much resistance on the part of the music industry itself. (Hal Zeiger: "I remember a conversation with M——D——, a very famous song-writer, who has written many of our all-time favorites, wherein he chided me for being involved with this kind of music and entertainment and I said to him, 'M——, you are just upset because it has been discovered and revealed that a song written by some young colored child in a slum area can capture the fancy of the American public more effectively than a song written by you, who lives in a Beverly Hills mansion'.")

Every year you could hear people saying, "I know it's only a phase…it'll poop out pretty soon. The big bands will come back." Year after year, the death of rock was predicted…a few times, as I recall, it was even officially announced. 'Rock 'n' roll is dead, calypso is all the rage…"

Oh, Those Great Rhythms; Digression 2

The function of the drums in a rock music ensemble is to keep the beat. ("It has a good beat…I give it 10 points. Dick.") On early R&B records, the drum part was usually executed with brushes. All the arrangement required, generally, was a dull thud on the second and fourth pulse of the bar. There were very few 'breaks' or 'fills'. When the drum fill (a short percussion outburst, usually at a cadence or resting point of a musical phrase) became popular in rock arrangements, it most often took the form of groups of triplets (three-note rhythmic figures, squeezed into the space of two beats…sounding like: ya-da-da ya-da-da ya-da-da ya-da-da-womp). For a while, during the mid 50s, it seemed like every record produced had one or more fills of this nature in it. Eventually, with the improvements in studios and recordings techniques, the drummers began to use sticks on the sessions and the cadence fills became more elaborate but, before and after the fill, the drummer's job was still to keep the beat…that same old crappy beat…the beat that made the kids hop around and scream and yell and buy records. A long process of rhythmic evolution has taken place since the early 50s. It is laughable now to think of that dull thud on the second and fourth as lewd and pulsating.

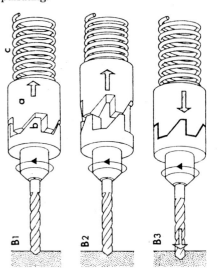

Green Visors

Hal Zeiger: "The problem at the time was basically this: trying to make the music acceptable, or, to try to get the right to expose it, and that took some doing. I knew the kids were listening to the radio stations...it was just a matter of how to merchandise this to get their dollars, too. I told Bill Graham (founder of the Fillmore and former manager of the Jefferson Airplane), 'You've got to understand when these things are underground, that's one thing. But the minute it goes over ground, the minute, you see, it looks like money, everyone wants in.'"

So to make R&B acceptable, the big shots of the record industry hired a bunch of little men with cigars and green visors, to synthesize and imitate the work of the Negroes. The visor men cranked out phony white rock. Highly skilled couriers then delivered the goods to American Bandstand along with a lot of presents (tokens of their esteem) to Dick Clark for all his marvelous assistance in the crusade to jam these products down the kids' throats. Pat Boone was notable, too, for his humanistic activities (bleaching Little Richard and making him safe for teenage consumption).

One of my favorite Negro R&B groups during the 40s was Hank Ballard and the Midnighters. Their work was some of the most important sociosexual true-to-life commentary of that era, for instance: '*Stingy Little Thing*' (a song in protest about girls who wouldn't 'put out'), '*Work With Me Annie*' and '*Annie Had A Baby*'. Songs like these got played on the air every once in a while – the kids would hear '*Annie Had A Baby*' and say, 'Hey, here's a song about a girl getting pregnant,' and rush to tune it in – but an official of the station (with teen-age children of his own to protect) would 'lay a pink memo on it,' and the song would sort of disappear."

The visor men, meanwhile, were magically purifying all this stuff. '*Work With Me Annie*' ('*Please don't cheat/Give me all my meat*') through the wisdom of their craft became 'Dance With Me, Henry' ('If you want romancin'/You better learn some dancin'").

Vaseline

White rock, overproduced and shiny, nearly slickened itself to death. (Remember Fats Domino with 'Strings'?) The music industry was slumping a bit. Was this to be the end of rock? Were we doomed to a new era of country & western tunes, smothered in Vaseline? Then, just in the nick of time, Beatlemania. New hope. There they were: cute, safe, white. The kids took to them immediately. Their music had real energy; it was sympathetic to their life style. It was music made for young people by other young people. No green visors. It seemed to radiate a secret message: 'You can be free. You can get away with it. Look, we're doing it!'

I'm sure the kids never really believed all The Beatles wanted to do was hold your hand. And the girls were provided with 'kissable closeups' (enlarged views of their idols' lips, teeth and gums) which they could kiss, touch, rub and/or hang on the bedroom wall. Girls forgot Elvis Presley. He was too greasy, too heavy business: sullen pouting and all that stuff. The Beatles were huggable and cute and moptops and happy and positive. Beatlemania was fun to be involved in.

The record companies were at a loss to compete with the British threat. Zeiger relates another droll incident: "I remember Mike Maitland who was then vice president and sales manager of Capitol Records. He was decrying the fact that they couldn't get any hit singles, and I said to him, 'Well, Mike, the reason is because you have the wrong people working for you'. 'Well, what do you want me to do? Get some of these fellows with the tight pants to produce these records?' I said, 'Exactly. Two button records can't be produced by guys with three button suits. It's all a matter of buttons.' Look at Mike Maitland now. He's president of Warner Brothers Records and look at the kind of thing they're putting out...fellows with tight pants...or no pants...are producing the records."

72 Tracks And Itchykoo Park; Digression 3

It might be interesting at this point to discuss the evolution of recording-studio techniques. In the very oldest of days, the recording engineer's main function was to stand behind the singer holding him by the shoulders, and either push him forward or pull him away from a large funnel-shaped object attached to a bent pin or something that used to function as a primitive microphone to gather sounds to be transcribed on a wax cylinder.

During the early stages of R&B, most recording was done on very large acetate discs. Then came tape. Monaural recordings gave way to stereo...then to three-track...then four-track. Four-track recording was the 'standard of the industry' for a while until some of those tight pants, no pants producers Zeiger mentioned put pressure on companies and manufacturers to obtain eight-track machines which would allow more creative freedom to the young musicians who were playing this wonderful new money-making form of music. Today, eight-track recording is common and the adventurous new breed of 'pop experimenters' are hustling to get 12-track machines, 16-track machines, 24-track machines (the Beatles, I hear, are setting up a nifty studio with 72 tracks).

Audience Education

There seems to be a trend in today's music toward eclecticism. The people who make this music are examining a wide range of possible musical and nonmusical elements to incorporate into their bags. Through rock music, the audience is being exposed to an assortment of advanced musical and electronic techniques that five years ago might have sent them screaming into the street. Amazing breakthroughs have been made in the field of 'audience education'.

These improvements have been made almost against the will of the mass media. Suppression for racial and sexual reasons doesn't go on as much but radio stations still do not program progressive rock in proportion to the market which exists for it. Specific songs which seem most threatening to the established order don't get on radio and TV. Example: 'Society's Child' by Janis Ian about interracial dating. (Mass media does more to keep Americans stupid than even the whole U.S. school system, that vast industry which cranks out trained consumers and technician-pawns for the benefit of other vast industries.) It is something of a paradox that companies which manufacture and distribute this art form (strictly for profit) might one day be changed or controlled by young people who were motivated to action by the products these companies sell.

The level of involvement with today's music is quite amazing. One example: Groupies. These girls, who devote their lives to pop music, feel they owe something personal to it, so they make the ultimate gesture of worship, human sacrifice. They offer their bodies to the music or its nearest personal representative, the pop musician. These girls are everywhere. It is one of the most amazingly beautiful products of the sexual revolution.

The Jimi Hendrix Phenomenon

Hendrix is one of the most revolutionary figures in today's pop culture, musically and sociologically. His success is a curious paradox in view of the historical prejudices outlined earlier.

Hendrix is 24 years old. He dropped out of a Seattle high school in the 11th grade. He was raised strictly by his parents: "They taught me to have manners." He is reasonably sincere and humble: "We are lucky to be listened to." He is apparently very happy with his commercial success. Partly because it allows him to act out some of his childhood fantasies (in his clothing for instance): "I always wanted to be a cowboy or a hadji baba or the Prisoner of Zenda..."

His strongest appeal is to the white female audience ranging in age from about 13 to 30, with the highest concentration of victims between 19 and 22. "I just carry advantages with me in my back pocket when I go off at a gig." His charisma also extends to a white male audience, 15 to 25.

He is realistic about his market appeal: "The black people probably talk about us like dogs...until we play." "When I see some of them in the street, they say. 'I see you got those two white boys with you.' I try to explain to them about all this new music. I play them some records. First I play Cream and when they say. 'Hey that's great, who is playing the guitar?' I tell them it's Eric Clapton and he's an Englishman. Then I might play them some of what we do. Sometimes they still think we're crazy."

Hendrix's music is very interesting. The sound of his music is extremely symbolic: orgasmic grunts, tortured squeals, lascivious moans, electric disasters and innumerable other audible curiosities are delivered to the sense mechanisms of the audience at an extremely high decibel level. In a live performance environment, it is impossible to merely listen to what the Hendrix group does...it eats you alive. (He is concerned about his live performance image: "I don't want everybody to solely think of us in a big flash of weaving and bobbing and groping, and maiming and attacking and...")

In spite of his maiming and groping, etc., the female audience thinks of Hendrix as being beautiful (maybe just a little scary), but mainly very sexy. The male audience thinks

of him as a phenomenal guitarist and singer. Boys will bring girls backstage for autographs. While signing their scraps of paper, shoulder blades, handbags and pants Hendrix will frequently be asked; "Do you think of any particular girl while you're playing, or do you just think of sex itself?" Meanwhile, the boys will ask, "What kind of equipment do you use? Do you get high before you go on stage?"

The boys seem to enjoy the fact that their girl friends are turned on to Hendrix sexually; very few resent his appeal and show envy. They seem to give up and say: "He's got it, I ain't got it, I don't know if I'll ever get it…but if I do, I wanna be just like him, because he's really got it." They settle for vicarious participation and/or buy a Fender Stratocaster, an Arbiter Fuzz Face, a Vox Wah-Wah Pedal, and four Marshall amplifiers.

The Gas Co., The Electric Co. & The Music Co; Digression 4

The loud sounds and bright lights of today are tremendous indoctrination tools. Is it possible to modify the human chemical structure with the right combination of frequencies? (Frequencies you can't hear are manifested as frequencies you can see in a light show.) Can prolonged exposure to mixed media produce mutations? If the right kind of beat makes you tap your foot, what kind of beat makes you curl your fist and strike? Do you cry if the violin is playing the melody molto vibrato?

Manifestations of response to music will vary according to the character of the music and the audience. Swooning to Kay Kyse is roughly equivalent to squealing for the Monkees or drooling over Jimi Hendrix. In each case the swoonee, squealee, or droolee is responding to the music in a manner which he feels is reasonably acceptable by current social standards in his peer group.

If you were drunk, and it was the middle of summer, Saturday night about 11.30, and you had your comfortable clothes on, and you were in a small beer joint dancing, and it's crowded (temperature about 112°), and the local Rock & Roll combo (Ruben and The Jets) is playing 'Green Onions' (or something that sounds just like it…all full of parallel fifths moving monotonously through a root progression I, IIb, IV, IIIb…or something like that, over and over again), and the guitar player goes to take a solo and stomps his fuzztone into action and turns his amplifier all the way up so his guitar squeals and screams and sounds absolutely vicious, and he bends

and mangles the strings and starts to really get it on, gyrating and going totally berserk and playing his ass off and everythin'…if you were drunk, and all this was going on, and you were out there dancing and sweating and really feeling the music (every muscle and fiber of your being etc., etc.) and the music suddenly got louder and more vicious…louder and viciouser than you could ever imagine (and you danced harder and got sweaty and feverish) and got your unsuspecting self worked up into a total frenzy, bordering on electric Buddha nirvana total acid freak cosmic integration (one with the universe), and you were drunk and hot and not really in control of your body or your senses (you are possessed by the music), and all of a sudden the music gets EVEN LOUDER…and not only that: IT GETS FASTER AND YOU CAN'T BREATHE. (But you can't stop either; it's impossible to stop) and you know you can't black out because it feels too good…I ask you now, if you were drunk and all this stuff is happening all over the place and somebody (with all the best intentions in the world) MADE YOU STOP so he could ask you this question: "Is a force this powerful to be overlooked by a society that needs all the friends it can get?" Would you listen?
Life Magazine.

Fig. 12

"Good Guitar Stuff" Or "Stereotypifications"? The Evolution Of The Guitar's Use In Pop Music; Brief Version

During the fifties it was rare to find a guitar solo on rock or R&B singles, it was usually the honk-squeak tenor sax syndrome taking up the space between the bridge and the third verse. When a guitar was heard (usually on the blues or country blues items I was collecting), its function bore little resemblance to today's collection of pathetic lick-spewage and freeze-dried stereotypifications. (All of you sensitive guitar fans who actually get off on our current pseudo-academic era of polished efficiency had better read another article.)

If you have access to them, take the time to listen to the guitar solos on 'Three Hours Past Midnight' (Johnny Guitar Watson), 'The Story Of My Life' (Guitar Slim), or just about any of B.B. King's singles from that period. For my taste, these solos are exemplary because what is being played seems honest and, in a musical way, a direct extension of the personality of the men who played them. If I were a music critic, I would have to say that these values for me mean more than the ability to execute clean lines or clouds of educated gnat-notes.

Other examples of good guitar stuff from that era might include 'Lucy Mae Blues' (Frankie Lee Simms), 'Happy Home' (Elmore James – even though Elmore tended to play the same famous lick on every record, I got the feeling that he meant it) and the work of Hubert Sumlin (and Buddy Guy a couple of times) on Howlin' Wolf's things. I'm sure there are other hot items, but this is a short article.

Also, to be fair about it, there were some classic examples of sterility then too in the kind of rock solos on the Bill Haley singles and the obnoxious kleen-teen finger work on the New York-based R&B vocal quintet records (on labels like Gee, on the up-tempo numbers with the ice-cream-cone chord changes)

Then we get to the Sixties. We get there partly because R&B was being produced to death (strings on Ray Charles and Fats Domino records) and because England was starting to ship back some recycled fifties music, played by people who were younger and cuter than the original performers, to be consumed by people who were younger and cuter than the original consumers (and who, especially in the case of Rolling Stones fans, had never heard the original recordings of

their revamped Slim Harpo/Muddy Waters repertoire…and not only that, folks, if they had heard the originals, they probably wouldn't have liked them at all, since neither of the original artists named above were as prance-worthy as Mick Jagger).

Obviously, part of the recycling process included the imitation of Chuck Berry guitar solos, B.B. King guitar solos, and even some abstractions of John Lee Hooker guitar solos. The guitar was becoming more prevalent in backing arrangements on singles, especially as a rhythm instrument. Solos on most white-person records of that day and age tended to be rhythmic also, especially in surf music. Almost everything that survives in popular memory (the greatest hits, in other words) was designed for the purpose of dancing – but mainly just to sell. The Sixties saw the beginnings of record production as a science in the service of commerce, with heavy emphasis on the repetition of successful formulas. The best that can be said about this period is that it brought us Jeff Beck at his feedback apex, Jimi Hendrix at his overkill-volume best, and Cream, which sort of legitimized jamming a lot onstage (so long as you could prove British descent, usually by reeling off musical quotations from blues records which most Americans had never heard).

(Radio programming nerds made sure you never heard any of that stuff because Negroes were playing it, and they did their best to protect the young audiences of the Fifties and early Sixties from such a horrible culture shock, while over in England the better musicians were lusting after vintage blues records, actually obtaining them, and having these records form the basis of their playing traditions).

So, briefly to review: I would characterize guitarism of the Fifties as having, in its best cases, some real humor, style, and personality, and, in its worst cases, mechanical sterility and lack of musical interest.

I would characterize the Sixties, as having, at its best, exploratory qualities not possible before the advent of heavy amplification and recording studio machinery; more rhythmic interest and, in some instances, real humor, style and personality. At its worst, the guitarism of the Sixties brought us amateur strummery; several swift kicks at the Fender Twin Reverb springs; the archetype of folk-rock 12-string swill (the predecessor of the horrible fake-sensitivity music we have today with the laid-back sensitive-type artist/singer/songwriter suffering person, posed against a wooden fence provided by the Warner Brothers Records art department,

graciously rented to all the other record companies who needed it for their version of the same crap); and the first examples of the 'psychedelic guitar solo,' not to mention Inna-Gadda-Da-Vida-ism.

Obviously this is condensing and leaving out a lot, but I'm sure that all of you entirely-too-modern persons who have read this far are getting anxious for something more relevant to your lifestyle – and you're absolutely right! A perspective of musical history has absolutely no place in today's thrilling musical world. Yes, that's right, you heard right!

How could any of this information be useful to a musical world that has reached a point of sophistication that accepts concepts like The Super-Group, The Best Guitar Player In The World, The Fastest Guitar Player In The World, The Prettiest Guitar Player In The World, The Loudest Guitar Player In The World, The Guitar Player In The World Who Has Collected The Most Oldest Guitars In The World (some of which have been played by dead guitar players who were actually musicians), and so forth?

The history of Pop Music has a habit of telling us who we really are – 'cause if we weren't that way, we wouldn't have spent billions of dollars on those records, would we? After careful training by media and merchandising people, the entire population (even guitar players) has been transmuted into a reasonably well-groomed odor-free, consumer-amoeba which is kept alive only to service those who run the industry and live by the motto, biggest, tastiest, loudest is most and best.

So, forget about the past; it means nothing to you now (unless you can find a way to play it louder/faster – which probably wouldn't be too hard since even infants today can play as fast as the earliest Mahavishnuisms). Let's face it, once you learn the 28 or 29 most commonly used rock guitar doodads (a few country licks, a little Albert King, a pentatonic scale here'n there, get yer heavy vibrato together) you are ready to live; to be what will be known in the future as 'The Guitar Player Of The Seventies.' Yes, soon you will belong to the ages, and when you've finally got your album contract, and it finally comes out, and it sells ten million copies, and when every beginning guitar player sits at home and hears you wanking away at phenomenal speed with your perfect fuzz and your thoroughly acceptable execution, and when that little guy with his first guitar (him and the ten million other ones) says to himself: "Shit, I can do that," and proceeds to memorize every awe-inspiring note, and then plays it faster than you…(maybe gets his 32nd notes up around a dotted whole note = 208). And not only that, after learning your solo faster, he transposes it up a minor third, steals some of his mother's clothes, gets a job in a bar, gets discovered, gets a record contract (with an advance ten times bigger than yours), makes an album (with a better budget than yours, because he's going to be the next big thing according to the executives at the record company, and they don't mind spending a little extra for real talent). And not only that, while you just figured out you can't play any faster because you haven't had any time to practise because you got coked out on the royalties of your first album(and you still have to record ten more according to your contract), and it's time to do your second album, and you've been asking recording engineers how a VSO works, meanwhile the little boy with his mother's clothes on gets his album out on the street, and it sells twenty million copies, and somewhere out there, there's twenty million other little guys with their first guitars, and they're listening to your recycled wank, and they're saying… (*Guitar Player*).

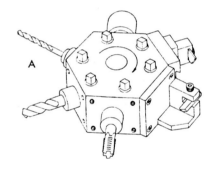

A

Two Orchestral Stupidities

Several years ago…five maybe…the people who promote our rock shows in Vienna (Stimmung Der Welt) approached me with the idea of doing a concert in Vienna with the Vienna Symphony. I said okay. After two or three years of pooting around with the mechanics of the deal, work began on the final preparations. The concert was to be funded by the City of Vienna, the Austrian Radio, the Austrian Television, and a substantial investment from me (the cost of preparing the scores and parts).

At the point when the official announcement was made that the concert would take place (I think it was in June or July), there was no written contract with any of the governmental agencies listed above. As it turned out, the person from the Austrian TV who pledged $300,000 toward the budget (which was to cover three weeks of rehearsal, shipping of our band equipment, air fares and housing for band members, and band and crew salaries…I was not getting paid for any of this) did not really have the authority to do so and was informed by his boss that that amount had already been committed to other TV projects. This created a situation wherein the remaining sponsors still had their funds available, and wished to proceed, but somebody had to round up the missing $300,000 from another source.

At this point Bennett Glotzer, my manager, got on a plane to Europe and spent the best part of a month thrashing around the continent trying to raise the missing bucks. No luck. Between his travel, food, hotels and intercontinental phone calls and my investment in copyist fees to prepare the music (not to mention the two or three years I had spent writing it), the total amount I had spent in cash at the time the concert was cancelled came to around $135,000…this is not funny unless you're Nelson Bunker Hunt.

That was orchestral stupidity number one…the second one goes like this: last year in Amsterdam, the head of The Holland Festival came to my hotel and said they wanted to do a special performance of my orchestral music with The Residentie Orchestra (from The Hague), as well as performances of certain other small pieces by The Nederlands Wind Ensemble, all of these performances were to take place during one whole week of the festival. I told him that I had received several offers in the past (including one from the Oslo Philharmonic where they thought they might be able to squeeze in two days of rehearsal), and described the whole Vienna business in glowing terms. I told him that it would be nice to have the music performed, but, since there was a lot of it, and it was difficult stuff, there was no way I would discuss it any further without the guarantee of a minimum of three weeks rehearsal, and in no way was I interested in spending any more of my own money on projects such as this.

It occurred to me that they were committed to doing the project, and that the rehearsal schedule could be arranged, and not only that…they were willing to pay for the WHOLE THING. The Holland Festival put up the equivalent of $500,000 for the event. Deals were then made with CBS to record and release the music, more copyists were hired, musicians from the U.S. who were going to play the amplified parts of the score were hired, road crew people who would handle the P.A. equipment (as the concert was to be held in an 8,000 seat hall) were hired, and a rock tour of Europe was booked (to help pay the cost of shipping the equipment and the salaries of the U.S. people involved…again, I was not getting paid), all in preparation for another summer orchestral concert that was doomed like the other one.

What happened? Well, first let's understand the economics of a project like this. It involves a lot of musicians and they all like to get paid (this is a mild way of putting it). Also, since it was to be an amplified concert, there is the problem of special equipment to make the sound as clear as possible in the hall (it was called 'THE AHOY'…a charming sort of Dutch indoor bicycle racing arena with a concrete floor and a banked wooden track all around the room). Also there was going to be a recording of the music, necessitating the expenditure of even more money for the rental of the equipment, engineer's salary, travel expense, etc., etc.

After making a deal with CBS to cover expenses that the Dutch government wouldn't, a new problem arose that became insurmountable – the needs of the U.S. musicians. Despite earnings of $15,000 for 17 weeks in Europe, all expenses paid, a few of these musicians called our office shortly before the start of U.S. rehearsals and tried to make secret deals to get their salaries raised and 'Don't tell the other guys…'

When I heard of this, I cancelled the usage of the electric group with the orchestra, saving myself a lot of time and trouble rehearsing them, and a lot of money moving them around. Plans remained in effect for the orchestral concerts to continue as acoustic events in smaller halls. The recording plans remained the same also…five days of recording following the live performances.

About a week or so after the attempted hijack by the U.S. musicians, our office received a letter from the head of the Residentie Orchestra. Among other things, it mentioned that the orchestra committee (a group of players that represents the orchestra members in discussions with the orchestra management) had hired a lawyer and were ready to begin negotiations to determine how much of a royalty they would get for making a record. Since I had already raised the funds from CBS to pay them the necessary recording scale for doing this work, such a demand seemed to be totally out of line with reality, as I had never heard of a situation wherein an orchestra demanded that the composer pay them royalties for their performance of works he had written, nor did I feel it would have been advisable to set a dangerous precedent that might affect the livelihood of other composers by acceding to the wishes of this greedy bunch of mechanics.

A short time after that, the orchestra manager and the guy we originally talked to from the Holland Festival flew to Los Angeles for a meeting to go over final details. They arrived at my house about midnight. By about 1.30 am , I had told them that I never wished to see their mercenary little ensemble and that permission to perform any of my works would not be granted to them under any circumstances. They left soon after that.

It was determined shortly thereafter that the cost of going through all of this intercontinental hoo-hah had brought my 'serious music investment' to about $250,000, and I still hadn't heard a note of it.

There you have it, folks…two orchestral stupidities, a conceptual double concert for inaudible instruments on two continents, perfectly performed by some of the most exceptional musicians of our time.

Musician 36.

Edgar Varèse, Idol Of My Youth. A Reminiscence And Appreciation

I have been asked to write about Edgar Varèse. I am in no way qualified to. I can't even pronounce his name right. The only reason I have agreed to is because I love his music very much, and if by some chance this article can influence more people to hear his works, it will have been worthwhile.

I was about thirteen when I read an article in *Look* about Sam Goody's Record Store in New York. My memory is not too clear on the details, but I recall it was praising the store's exceptional record merchandising ability. One example of brilliant salesmanship described how, through some mysterious trickery, the store actually managed to sell an album called '*Ionization*' (the real name of the album was '*The Complete Works of Edgar Varèse, Volume One*'). The article described the record as a weird jumble of drums and other unpleasant sounds.

I dashed off to my local record store and asked for it. Nobody ever heard of it. I told the guy in the store what it was like. He turned away, repulsed, and mumbled solemnly. "I probably wouldn't stock it anyway...nobody here in San Diego would buy it."

I didn't give up. I was so hot to get that record I couldn't even believe it. In those days I was a rhythm-and-blues fanatic. I saved any money I could get (sometimes as much a $2 a week) so that every Friday and

Saturday I could rummage through piles of old records at the Juke Box Used Record Dump (or whatever they called it) in the Maryland Hotel or the dusty corners of little record stores where they'd keep the crappy records nobody wanted to buy.

One day I was passing a hi-fi store in La Mesa. A little sign in the window announced a sale of 45's. After shuffling through their singles rack and finding a couple of Joe Houston records, I walked toward the cash register. On my way I happened to glance into the L.P. bin. Sitting in the front, just a little bent at the corners, was a strange-looking black and white album cover. On it there was a picture of a man with a gray frizzy hair. He looked like a mad scientist. I thought it was great that somebody had finally made a record of a mad scientist. I picked it up. I nearly (this is true, ladies and gentlemen) peed in my pants...THERE IT WAS! EMS 401. *The Complete Works of Edgar Varèse Volume 1...*Intégrales, Density 21.5, Ionization, Octandre...Rene Le Roy, the N.Y. Wind Ensemble, the Juilliard Percussion Orchestra, Fredenc Waldman Conducting...Inner notes by Sidney Finkelstein, WOW!

I ran over to the singles box and stuffed the Joe Houston records back in it. I fumbled around in my pocket to see how much money I had (about $3.80) I knew I had to have a lot of money to buy an album. Only old people had enough money to buy albums. I'd never bought an album before. I sneaked over to the guy at the cash register and asked him how much EMS 401 cost, "That gray one in the box? $5.95".

I had searched for that album for over a year and now...disaster. I told the guy I only had $3.80. He scratched his neck. "We use that record to demonstrate the hi-fi's with, but nobody ever buys one when we use it...you can have it for $3.80 if you want it that bad."

I couldn't imagine what he meant by "demonstrating hi-fi's with it," I'd never heard a hi-fi, I only knew that old people bought them. I had a genuine lo-fi...it was a little box about 4 inches deep with imitation wrought-iron legs at each corner (sort of brass-plated) which elevated it from the table top because the speaker was in the bottom. My mother kept it near the ironing board. She used to listen to a 78 of The Little Shoemaker on it. I took off the 78 of The Little Shoemaker and carefully moving the speed lever to 33 ⅓ (it had never been there before), turned the volume all the way up and placed the all-purpose Osmium-tip needle in the lead-in spiral to Ionization. I have a nice Catholic mother who likes Roller Derby. Edgar Varèse does not get her off, even to this very day. I was forbidden to play that record in the living room ever again.

In order to listen to The Album, I had to stay in my room. I would sit there every night and play it two or three times and read the liner notes over and over. I didn't understand them at all. I didn't know what timbre was. I never heard of polyphony. I just like the music because it sounded good to me. I would force anybody who came over to listen to it. (I had heard someplace that in radio stations the guys would make chalk marks on records so they could find an exact spot, so I did the same thing to EMS 401…marked all the hot items so my friends wouldn't get bored in the quiet parts.

I went to the library and tried to find a book about Mr. Varèse. There wasn't any. The librarian told me he probably wasn't a Major Composer. She suggested I look in books about new or unpopular composers. I found a book that had a little blurb in it (with a picture of Mr. Varèse as a young man, staring into the camera very seriously) saying that he would be just as happy growing grapes as being a composer.

On my fifteenth birthday my mother said she'd give me $5. I told her I would rather make a long-distance phone call. I figured Mr. Varèse lived in New York because the record was made in New York (and because he was so weird, he would live in Greenwich Village). I got New York Information, and sure enough, he was in the phone book.

His wife answered. She was very nice and told me he was in Europe and to call back in a few weeks. I did. I don't remember what I said to him exactly, but it was something like: "I really dig your music." He told me he was working on a new piece called Deserts. This thrilled me quite a bit since I was living in Lancaster, California, then. When you're fifteen and living in the Mojave Desert and find out that the world's greatest composer, somewhere in a secret Greenwich Village laboratory, is working on a song about your 'home town' you can get pretty excited. It seemed a great tragedy that nobody in Palmdale or Rosamond would care if they ever heard it. I still think Deserts is about Lancaster, even if the liner notes on the Columbia LP say it's something more philosophical.

All through high school I searched for information about Varèse and his music. One of the most exciting discoveries was in the school library in Lancaster. I found an

orchestration book that had score examples in the back, and included was an excerpt from Offrandes with a lot of harp notes (and you know how groovy harp notes look). I remember fetishing the book for several weeks.

When I was eighteen I got a chance to go to the East Coast to visit my Aunt Mary in Baltimore. I had been composing for about four years then but had not heard any of it played. Aunt Mary was going to introduce me to some friend of hers (an Italian gentleman) who was connected with the symphony there. I had planned on making a side trip to mysterious Greenwich Village. During my birthday telephone conversation, Mr. Varèse had casually mentioned the possibility of a visit if I was ever in the area. I wrote him a letter when I got to Baltimore, just to let him know I was in the area.

I waited. My aunt introduced me to the symphony guy. She said "This is Frankie. He writes orchestra music". The guy said, "Really? Tell me, sonny boy, what's the lowest note on the bassoon?" I said, "B flat…and also it says in the book you can get 'em up to a C or something in the treble clef." He said, "Really? You know about violin harmonics?" I said, "What's that?" He said "See me again in a few years."

I waited some more. The letter came. I couldn't believe it. A real handwritten letter from Edgar Varèse! I still have it in a little frame. In very tiny scientific looking script it says:

VII 12th/57
Dear Mr. Zappa,
I am sorry not to be able to grant your request. I am leaving for Europe next week and will be gone until next spring. I am hoping however to see you on my return. With best wishes
Sincerely
Edgar Varèse

I never got to meet Mr. Varèse. But I kept looking for records of his music. When he got to be about eighty I guess a few companies gave in and recorded some of his stuff. Sort of a gesture. I imagine. I always wondered who bought them besides me. It was about seven years from the time I first heard his music till I met someone else who even knew he existed. That person was a film student at USC. He had the Columbia LP with Poème électronique on it. He thought it would make groovy sound effects.

I can't give you any structural insights or academic suppositions about how his music works or why I think it sounds so good. His

music is completely unique. If you haven't heard it yet, go hear it. If you've already heard it and think it might make groovy sound effects, listen again.
FZ 1971

My Favourite Records

If you want to learn how to play guitar, listen to Wes Montgomery. You also should go out and see if you can get a record by Cecil Taylor if you want to learn how to play the piano.

You ought to look into the complete works of Anton Webern on Columbia (K4L-232), conducted by Robert Craft. That's four records. Robert Craft is not always an excellent conductor, and his performances are not always absolutely accurate, but they probably didn't give him a very good budget because it was modern music, and they wanted to get the job over with, and he was probably under pressure, so don't mind the mistakes that are on there if you're following it with a score.

Also, Pièrre Boulez conducts his own composition. Le Marteau Sans Maître. I don't know what label that's on, but it's the one with Boulez conducting. The one by Robert Craft has too many mistakes.

Also you ought to get Bartok's first, second and third piano concertos, which are all very groovy and good to dance to. I have the version on Westminster (18277) by Edith Farnadi with the Vienna State Opera Orchestra. I've never heard any other version of the second and third piano concertos so I don't know whether or not that's the best recording. It might not even be available. I heard another version of the first at Andy Kulberg's, of the Blues Project, who has an extensive collection of modern music.

Also, buy everything that you can by Igor Stravinsky and dance to it – especially L'Histoire Du Soldat, which means Soldier's Tale, and the Agon Ballet, which is a beautiful thing.

There's a record by Kadhenz Stockhausen on the Deutsche Gramophon label called 'Gesang der Jungling'. It's the Song Of The Youths, Kontackte contract) is on the other side. Buy that. (DGG 138811)

I hope you spell all the names right because if any of these composers read *Hit Parade*, and see a mistake, they're going to be real mad at you. FZ 1967.

F.Z, Pièrre Boulez.

The Complete History Of The Last Few Weeks Of The Mothers Of Invention

'Hot Rats/Grand Wazoo'

The following text was intended for the 'Grand Wazoo' tour programme (September 1972). This was not completed and Warner's promotional bulletin was issued later (Reprise circular, vol 4, No 40, October 9, 1972). Meanwhile Zappa left on a tour of the U.S. and Canada with nine musicians, a Mothers style band called The Grand Wazoo, who played a completely new set. There were new arrangements of older pieces like 'Mr. Green Genes', and previously unheard compositions like 'Rollo', 'Father O'Blivion' and 'Cosmik Debris' (with lyrics).

The Mothers Of Invention, 'Hot Rats/Grand Wazoo'

Right from the early days of The Mothers (roughly from 1964), I was interested in forming a sort of electric orchestra, – an orchestra capable of performing difficult compositions with an intensity of sound normally associated with pop music. The formation of the new MOI/HR/GW is the first large scale effort to get such a monstrosity together, and travel with it across a few continents giving concerts. The Wazoo first appeared on September 10, 1972 at the Hollywood Bowl. On September 13, they left for a trip through Berlin, London, La Haye, New York and Boston, and finally came back to L.A. on September 25. There were eight concerts altogether.

If it turns out that this inaugural tour is anything other than a financial catastrophe (the production, transportation and travelling expenses for such a large band are extremely high), The Wazoo will return for another series of concerts next summer. In any case, The Wazoo will be solemnly disbanded after the Boston concert. Immediately after I return to L.A. rehearsals will begin for another kind of MOI...a group of ten, who will tour Canada and the U.S. at the end of the year, and will be playing an entirely new

repertoire. But until then, here are some details about The Wazoo...

Every 'new' group (and even some of the old ones when they can) publishes some sort of profession of faith, explaining their fantastic potential and the pleasures that will arise when they show off their unique material, their unlimited stagemanship and/ or their good vibrations. Usually all this is accompanied by a description of their wonderful on-stage freedom and, to crown it all, how much everyone in the band loves what they are doing and what a good, healthy bunch of guys they are. Even if they're not healthy, they may be nasty and degenerate, you can be sure that despite it all each of them has an extraordinary talent, a heart of gold and a sensitive soul. This can be seen from the band's photo and their pained, innocent or distraught faces.

I claim nothing of the kind concerning The Wazoo. In such marketing operations there should be one or two paragraphs stating that no-one in the group really cares about money, followed by a carefully formulated declaration of the new band's intention of making the world a better place to live through its music (which is so sensitive, so inexpressibly deep...or maybe it is just intended to be a vibrant chorus, sung to communicate gigantic amounts of energy to the happy audience, or something like that).

For those who are interested, the MOI/ HR/GW will be offering, for a short period, a musical alternative to the attitudes I have been discussing, which could also be called 'green limousine consciousness'.

In fact, The Wazoo cannot really be compared with any other previous rock 'n' roll outfit. It consists of twenty musicians, most of whom sit and read music off neat rows of charming wooden stands. None of them sing. None of them dance; they only play music.

The MOI/HR/GW comprises:
Frank Zappa (*guitar, white conductor's baton with cork handle*),
Tony Duran (*slide guitar*),
Ian Underwood (*piano and synthesizer*),
Dave Parlato (*bass*),
Jerry Kessler (*electric cello*),
Jim Gordon (*electric drums*),
Mike Atshul (*piccolo, bass clarinet and other wind instruments*),
Jay Migliori (*flute, tenor sax and others*),
Earl Dummler (*oboe, double bass, sarrusophone and others*),
Ray Reed (*clarinet, tenor sax and others*),

Charles Owens (*soprano sax, alto sax and others*),
Joanne McNabb (*bassoon*),
Malcom McNabb (*d-trumpet*),
Sal Marquez (*b-flat trumpet*),
Tom Malone (*b-flat trumpet, tuba*),
Glen Ferris (*trombone*),
Kenny Shroyer (*trombone*),
Tom Raney (*vibes and electric percussion*) and
Ruth Underwood (*marimba and electric percussion*).

We will be playing the same set at each of the eight concerts. The pieces are 'New Brand Clouds', 'Big Swifty', 'Approximate', 'For Clavin And His Next Two Hitch-Hikers', 'Think It Over', 'Low Budget Dog Meat (medley)' and 'The Adventures Of Greggery Peccary'; as an encore (everybody plays encores and even if nobody mentions them) 'Variant Processional March' and 'Penis Dimension'. All of these compositions have room for improvisation, except 'Low Budget Dog Meat', which is made up of a selection of recognizable themes from 'Music For Low Budget Orchestra', 'The Dog Breath Variations' and 'Uncle Meat'.

The concert will be performed in a relaxed, tolerably direct and non-theatrical style. Only a few members of The Wazoo are used to playing popular music or are able to function safely if disguised by fringes, leaves and tinsel. Stage clothes are left to the individual's choice at the risk of critics dismissing The Wazoo's public image as 'monotonous and non-existent'.

Those among the audience who have a fetishistic desire to occupy one of the front seats in order to be able to examine more closely the group's ability to squint and pull faces (to see whether they are really up to date) will be disappointed to note that the eyeballs of The Wazoo's musicians are fixed either on the printed music or on the conductor's baton. Our one concession to such tomfoolery is putting Earl Dummler in the front row of the wind section, so that for the first time you can contemplate a grown man with a fashionable hairstyle battling with the forces of nature in order to wring the right note out of a sarrusophone, a modified double bass in E flat. In direct contrast to the misty legends that surround the birth of your 'average supergroup', the story behind our Wazoo is rather boring. I wanted a brass section for the orchestra, so I called the trombonist Ken Shroyer, who I had already worked with on 'Lumpy Gravy'. Kenny was The Wazoo's musical contractor. With a dog-eared copy of the local Musicians Union Directory, Shroyer managed to fill the empty spaces by picking up his telephone and grunting sentences like: 'Does this interest you?' 'Can you read music?', 'Do you have time to practise?' and the recurrent punchline, 'Are you free to go on tour?'

Thanks to Shroyer's irreproachable diplomacy, The Wazoo has probably earned its place in the Rock and Roll Hall of Fame, for the simple reason that it is the only 'new' group in rock history which has known from the start that it will not be as successful as The Beatles, and has also known throughout its history the exact time and place that it will split up: after the Boston show, in the dressing room, on September 24.

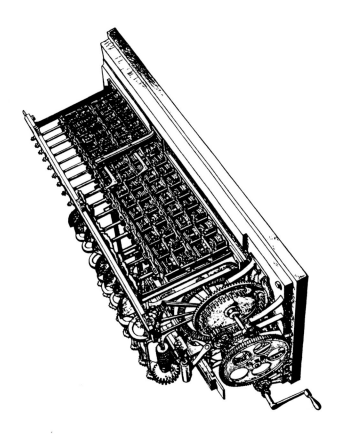

The Music

'The New Brand Clouds'

In theory, this piece should have appeared at the end of the set because it comes from the last act of *'Greggery Peccary'*. It will be played first for a number of reasons:

1. It's not a bad opening number.
2. As you have never heard *'The Adventures Of Greggery Peccary'* before, you won't be upset if it doesn't come at the end and it will not make you boo.
3. At the beginning there is a version of the 'Billy The Mountain' theme, so you could see a conceptual link with our last concert (if that sort of thing appeals to you).
4. It is the first piece The Wazoo learnt, so for nostalgic reasons it could also be the first one you hear us play. (For more information see the note on *'The Adv. Of G. Peccary'*).

'Big Swifty'

This piece *(the entire first side of the album Hot Rats-Waka/Jawaka)* consists of a theme made up of a rapid sequence of variations, some solos and an out-chorus, arranged like a ballroom orchestra and supported by an open rhythmical structure in 4/4. The theme's new form has its origins in a guitar solo off the album which Sal Marquez transcribed. After about an hour of orchestral improvisation, Sal managed to transcribe this rhythmically confusing piece of music. (I can't do this sort of musical dictation but Marquez can, thanks to his boring education at the University of North Texas.) After he had written it down, we added three more trumpets and hey presto! A more organised ending to 'Big Swifty'.

The arrangement of the theme here is more harmonic and has a number of orchestral improvements on the original (like the addition of a woodwind section and percussion in passages which on the record are played only on guitar and trumpet). It is not 'just like the record', but you'll see.

'Approximate'

In this selection each musician can choose the tone pitch they want to play. In the whole piece, there are only a few bars in which pitch is indicated (and these are introduced for the sake of contrast). The rest of the score is made up of triplets and crotchets linked by little 'X's. These are markers which show by their positions the approximate register for each instrument. The piece can be performed by any number of musicians greater than four. The general pattern is a single part that corresponds to all the instruments in C and F (including percussion). To this, another single part is added for instruments in B flat and E flat. The electric bass and the bass drum have separate parts which are nonetheless linked to the others.

'For Calvin'.

This piece is dedicated to Calvin Schenkel, who has been my friend for several years, and who is responsible for the graphic/visual side of the MOI, from the album covers to the cartoon sequences in *'200 Motels'*, including the advertising. We have already recorded this track for the *'Grand Wazoo'* album, soon to be released. There are words, but in concert we will play an instrumental version…the lyrics tell the story of a mysterious 'Fairy Morgana' whom he meets on his way to work, and are rather hard to explain, but perhaps you can use your imagination to invent a story, given the text:

Where did they go?
Where did they come from?
What has become of them now?

How much was the leakage
From the drain in the night
And who are those dudes
In the back seat of Calvin's car?

Where did they go
When they got off the car?
Did they go get a sandwich
And eat it in the dark?
Where did they go
With the waxed-paper bundles
When the sandwiches vanished
And the crumbs fell all over?

Where did they go?
Where did they come from?
Where d'ya think they're gonna
Re-appear tomorrow?

'Think It Over'. (The Grand Wazoo).

About six weeks ago, I finished the script for a science-fiction musical comedy called *'Hunchentoot'* (maybe it will never be staged). This piece is part of it, and is sung by an industrial knight who is fanatically religious about the future, to initiate his supporters who are meditating under the influence of Alpha Waves:

If something gets in your way
Just think it over…
And…it will fall down, etc.

But here, it is an instrumental piece, presented in *'Grand Wazoo'* camouflage. There's no scientific explanation for this, it is simply a shuffle.

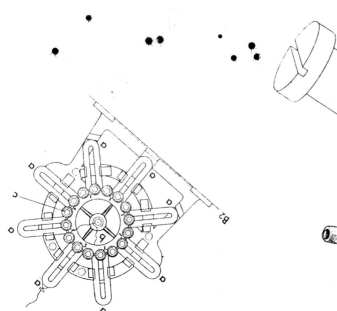

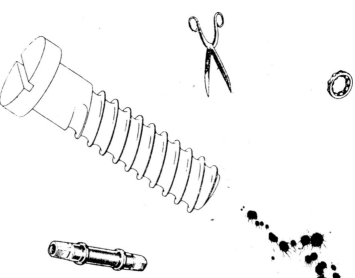

'Low Budget Dog Meat'.

This selection contains themes from three previously recorded tracks. The arrangement has some difficult instrumental passages, and some of them are not always played perfectly (but why the hell should they be?), in particular the high trombone part at the beginning, the section for electric piano and marimba in the second part, and the frisky, jangling theme in the last bit, which has presented some problems, as has the new synthesizer. Malcom McNabb's trumpet should surprise you throughout the second part with its high, cawing sound.

'The Adventures Of Greggery Peccary'.

'The Adventures Of Greggery Peccary' have their place alongside the film *'Uncle Meat'*, the legendary history of the original MOI as a nine record set, and more recently, the *'Hunchentoot'* project, as pieces which may never see the full light of day. It was originally conceived as a ballet with recitation telling the adventures of a little pig who belongs to a doomed race. Not much potential in this idea.

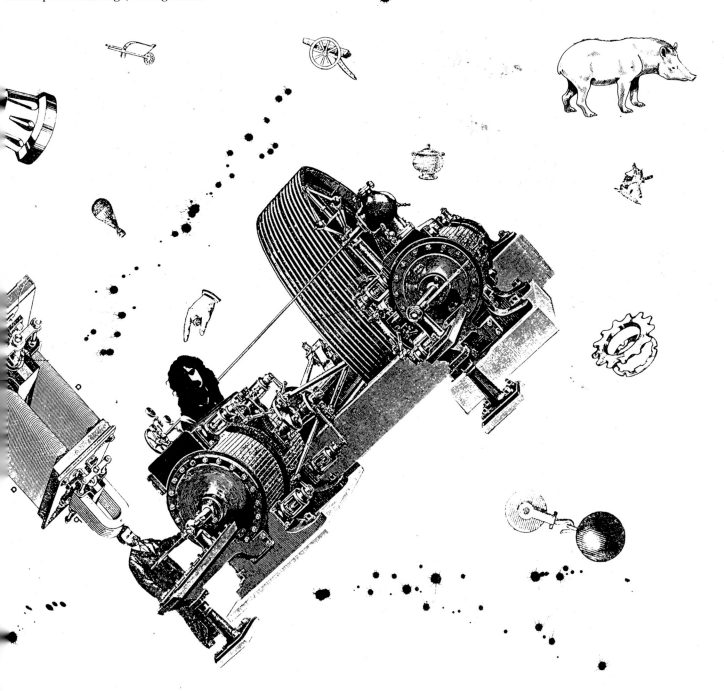

Articles Written By Frank Zappa

'The Oracle Has It All Psyched Out'. *Life*, June 1968.
'My Favorite Records'. *Hit Parader*, 1967.
'The Complete History Of The MOI/Hot Rats/Grand Wazoo'. Warner promo-circular, No 40 Vol 4, 1972.
''50s Teenagers And '50s Rock'. *Evergreen*, August 1970.
'Groupies As People'. *High Times* 82 interview, 1969 (tape).
'Edgar Varèse, Idol Of My Youth'. *Stereo Review*, June 1971.
'Two Orchestral Stupidities'. *Musician' 36*, Sept-Oct 1981.
Articles in *Guitar Player*. 'Absolutely Frank', 'First Steps In Odd Meters', 'Putting Some Garlic In Your Playing', 'Non-Foods', 'Stepping Outside The Beat', 'Coming To Grips With Polyrhythms', 'Good Guitar Stuff And Stereotypifications', 'The Evolution Of The Guitar Used In Pop Music: Brief Version', 'The Incredible Story Of The Mothers, Zappa on Watson'.
     There are also a number of booklets that came with albums:
'*Absolutely Free*', '*Uncle Meat Libretto*', '*Burnt Weeny Sandwich*', '*200 Motels*', '*You Are What You Is, (Say Cheese)*'.
     Letter to Ronald Reagan, August 29, 1985.
     "Extortion Pure and Simple – An Open Letter to the Music Industry" *Cash Box* guest editorial.
Statement to the Congress of the U.S.A. 19th September, 1985.

Books About Frank Zappa

Zapzapzappa, Rolf Ulrich Kaiser, Kinder der Geburtagpresse, Koln, 1969.
Frank Zappa, Rolf Ulrich Kaiser, Hoorn, Holland, 1971.
No Commercial Potential, David Walley, Outerbridge and Lazard, New York, 1972. Second Edition, EP Dutton, 1980.
Frank Zappa Et Les Mothers Of Invention, Alain Dister, Editions Albin Michel, Paris 1975.
Good Night Boys And Girls, Michael Gray, England 1975.
Alla Zappa, Urban Gweder, Ed Bucherkarawane, Adliswill, Switzerland, 1976.
Plastic People Songbuch/Corrected Copy, C. Weissner & Zappa, 2001, Verlag, Frankfurt, 1977.
The Zappalog, Norbert Obermanns, Germany, 1981.
Zappa (é più duro di tuo Marito), Massimo Bassoli, Gammalibri, Milan '82.
F.Z. lyrics translated into Italian with an introduction by Riccardo Bertoncelli, Arcana, Italy.
Mother Is The Story Of Frank Zappa, Michael Gray, Proteus, England, 1985.

Books Written By Frank Zappa

Them Or Us (The Book), Barfko-Swill, PO box 5418, North Hollywood, Ca 91616-5418.
This was written to answer the question of how several very different things could be linked together to form an even greater absurdity. It is a story and screen-play, not a rock biography. It was originally to be called '*Christmas In New Jersey*'. '*Them Or Us*' tells of Francesco Zappa, and gives Frank's unorthodox opinions on Mozart and David Bowie. It also discusses '*Sofa*', '*Billy The Mountain*', '*Big Swifty*', '*Greggery Peccary*','*Hunchentoot*', '*Thingfish*', '*Joes's Garage*' and '*Drakma*'. Characters from throughout the complete works are united in totally mind-boggling 300 page script.

The Guitar Book, Milwin Music, 8112 Bluemond Road, Milwaukee, Wisconsin 53213. This is 300 pages of written guitar solos from the albums '*Shut Up 'N' Play Yer Guitar*', '*You Are What You Is*', '*Joe's Garage Acts 2 & 3*', '*Sheik Yerbouti*' and '*Zoot Allures*'.
Frank also published musical scores of his earlier period in *The Frank Zappa Song Book, Vol I*, Big 3, L.A., 1973.

Fanzines

Mother's Home Journal, Graig Pinkus, 1972-3.
Hot Ratz Times, (11 numbers, 1973-5), Urban Gweder.
The Life And Times Of Frank Zappa, London.
A remake of '*Ten Years On The Road*' to celebrate a decade of The Mothers.
Zappa y Madres, Gaspar Fraga, Barcelona.
Totally Zapped, 13 numbers, U.S.A.
Mother People, PO Box 1056, Orange Connecticut 06477, U.S.A.
Absolutely Free Newsletter, c/o Obermanns, Unterbuchstr, 4048 Grevenbroisch, Germany.
Society Pages, F.Z. Society, Box 5211, Majorstua 0303, Oslo 3, Norway.
L'Oeil de Zappa, (5 photocopied numbers, 1 offset). 1980-81, Nanterre, France.
Black Page (Holland), *Cucamonga* (Holland) and *Dancin' Fool* (Germany) are recent small cirulation fanzines.

Zappa Products

Zappa has his own official distribution outlet, where you can obtain a variety of products such as the '*Dub Room*' video, rare albums such as '*Baby Snakes*', re-editions such as the '*Old Masters*', T-shirts, musical scores of his work and the book '*Them Or Us*'. Telephone: 1818 786 7546. Address: Barfko-Swill, Box 5418, North Hollywood, CA 91616-5418, U.S.A.

Filmography

RUN HOME SLOW, 1959
Produced by Don Cerveris and Tim Sullivan. Zappa wrote th music. It includes a recognizable version of '*Duke Of Prune* which is adapted for '*Absolutely Free*', 1966.

THE WORLD'S GREATEST SINNER, 1961
By Tim Carey. It contains an early hint of '*Holiday In Berlin* ('*Burnt Weeny Sandwich*), which recurs throughout th score and was written by Zappa.

BURNT WEENY SANDWICH, 1970
A short piece of film which was never released and was on shown once, at the San Fernando State College.

UNCLE MEAT, 1970
Never released because of financial problems. Only the mus remains on the album.

200 MOTELS, 1971
Surrealistic documentary. Cast include Ringo Star Theodore Bikel, Keith Moon, Jim Carl Black, Martin Licker Janet Ferguson, Miss Lucy, Dick Barber, Pamela Miller an The Mothers Of Invention. It was produced by Zappa, wh also composed the music which is performed by the Roy Philharmonic, conducted by Holgar Howarth, guit ensemble led by John Williams. Shot entirely on video l Tony Palmer, then transferred to 35mm.

BABY SNAKES, 1979
'A film about people who do stuff that is not normal.'
It lasts 2 hours 43 minutes. Premier was December 21, 197 at Victoria Theater, New York. Awarded Premier Grand pr for musical film, Paris 1981. Features Adrian Belew, Ter Bozzio, Bruce Brickford and Roy Estrada.

Zappa's Appearances In Films And Documentaries

1965. MONDO HOLLYWOOD. Documentary on t Hollywood Freak scene.
1967. THE MONKEES. Zappa is interviewed by M Nesmith.
1967. HEAD. Another Monkees film. Zappa appears as critic.
1969. MUSIC POWER. A film by Jerome Laperrousa showing the festival at Amougies, October 1969. Zappa, presenter, jams with Pink Floyd, Aynsley Dunbar and Arcl Shepp.
1970. VPROTV. A Dutch documentary showing Zappa home, in the studio and in concert.

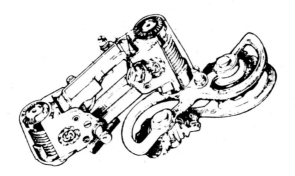

Videos

In 1982, Zappa completed a 90 minute video called *Dub Room*, which contains most of the famous 1974 TV show with Napoleon Murphy Brock, Ruth Underwood, Tom Fowler, George Duke and Chester Thompson. This is interspersed with previously unreleased recordings of the 1981 band – Steve Vai, Ed Mann and Chad Wackerman. There are also animated extracts from '*Baby Snakes*', by Bruce Brickford. Zappa made video clips for '*Mudd Club*', '*Bobby Brown*' and especially '*You Are What You Is*', which was banned in the U.S.A. because it contained a Reagan look-alike. The TV show *A Token Of His Extreme* (1975), recorded at KCET Studios in December 1974, was also censored in the U.S.A. but has been shown several times on TV in Europe. The first time was in France (Juke-Box, Freddie Hauser). Here is a list of Zappa's most notable TV appearances:

1968.   21 October, French TV channel one, 10 mins.
1970.   'VPRO-TV'. Holland, 1 hour.
1973.   Stockholm, 50 mins.
1974.   KCET special, *A Token Of His Extreme*, 55 mins.
1976.   *Saturday Night Live* (with John Belushi and Don Pardo), U.S.A., 12 mins.
1978.   *Sverige Magasin*, Sweden, 24 mins.
1978.   *Cadillac Extravaganza*, Austria, 30 mins.
1978.   *We Don't Mess Around*, Munich, 1 hour.
1979.   *Make Me Laugh*, Germany, 8 mins.
1980.   *Live From Palais Des Sports*, Paris, 2 hours.
1980.   *More Than A Concert*, Holland, 55 mins.
1980.   *At The Mudd Club*, NY, U.S.A., 35 mins.
1981.   MTV live broadcast by satellite. U.S.A., 100 mins.
1983.   *Sounds*, Australia, 40 mins.

This does not include individual song performances or TV interviews of less than 8 mins.

Other Zappa videos: DUMB ALL OVER, 47 minutes, intended exclusively for TV networks; YOU ARE WHAT YOU IS, 1 hour; THE TORTURE NEVER STOPS (*The Frank Zappa Concert That Knocked The Crowd Silly*), 120 mins, distributed by LBS Video/777 Third Avenue, NY, New York 10017.

The following videos became available in 1985: *200 Motels*, Warner home video, 96 mins; *Does Humor Belong In Music?* (F.Z. live in New York), EMI Picture Music Stereo, 57 mins; *Baby Snakes, Barfko-Swill; Dub Room* is also available from Barfko; *Talking With Frank Zappa*, 34 mins; Anti-drug video done with Pennsylvania State Police.

Musical Comedies

HUNCHENTOOT, 1972.
In the summer of 1972, Zappa wrote a science-fiction script intended to be set to music and shown on Broadway. He prepared illustrations for the costumes, stage instructions and a musical score. The final script had 81 pages of which 72 were the story and the rest production notes. It had a cast of forty two, including musicians. The choir consisted of three sopranos, two altos, one tenor, two baritones and two basses. The orchestra included a wind section of five, a woodwind section of six, an electric string section of four, two percussionists, one player of various keyboards, one guitarist (six and twelve string, plus mandolin), one bassist (acoustic and electric) and one drummer. The central character is Drakma, a cosmic she-devil who lives on an unknown planet and wants to invade Earth. The stage is divided into four: to the right is Earth, with its headquarters represented by a table, seven chairs and a brick wall with posters stuck on it. Drakma's planet is to the left, and consists of a big purple sofa, a small mountain with a cave, a pink hair-drier and some paper-maché volcanos which give out smoke. The orchestra is in the centre and the choir is behind Earth's Headquarters, cut off by a sheet of glass. A giant screen is stretched over the orchestra.

The story is in two parts. At the start, the orchestra plays the Overture, and the narrator introduces the characters. Then Drakma appears singing '*Time Is Money*' (from the album '*Sleep Dirt*'). She tells Hunchentoot her plan, and wins over the Spider of Destiny ('*Sleep Dirt*'). Then they dance and sing '*Think It Over*' ('*Grand Wazoo*'), which is followed by '*Hunchentoot Blues*'. '*Maximum Potential*' is a hymn to the Spider. Part one ends with '*Flambay*' ('*Sleep Dirt*'). Act 2 consists of '*Prelude To Act 2*' and '*Hunchentoot The Pimp*'.

Drakma's adventures have never been staged, but there is a version of them in the book '*Them Or Us*'.

THINGFISH 1984

In April 1984 Zappa published an extract of twenty one pages plus colour photos from '*Thingfish*' in the American pornographic magazine *Hustler*. The entire work came out in a boxed set that autumn, starring Johnny Guitar Watson, Terry and Dale Bozzio, Ike Willis, Ray White and Napoleon Murphy Brock.

'*Thingfish*' is a musical comedy about the musical comedy, and opens as a Broadway style musical before turning into an American sexual Theatre Of The Absurd. A trendy young couple are followed through a series of adventures while the scene shifts from Broadway to Quentin Robert de Nameland's Video Chapel and the Alladin Hotel, Las Vegas, among others. Harry, the husband, has a flashback to when he was traumatised by the *Women's Liberation Movement* and flirted with homosexuality before falling for a plastic replica of his wife. She is disgusted and has sex with a giant briefcase. The host cum co-ordinator, Thingfish, speaks in a Southern Black accent, exaggerated so that it sounds like imitators from Harlem or white people trying to be cool. The characters are often inspired by the TV show *Amos And Andy* (1952), which featured George 'Kingfish' Stevens played by Tim Moore. One of his partners, Algonquin J. Calhoun, becomes Sister Owl Gonkwin Jane Cowhoon in '*Thingfish*'. It is written to be performed, but is available only on record, and is alluded to in the book *Them Or Us*.

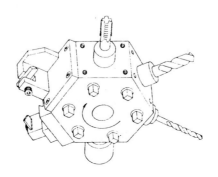

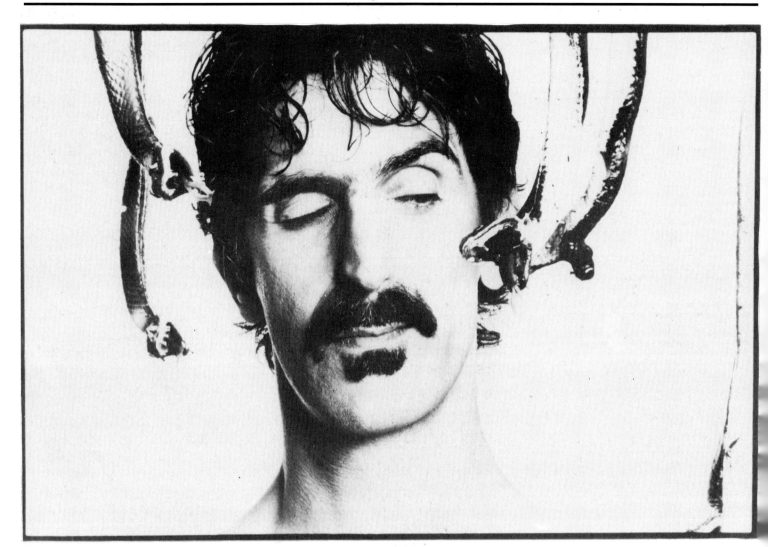

Discography

45 rpm

1966	*'How Could I Be Such A Fool'/'Help, I'm A Rock'*
	'It Can't Happen Here'/'Help I'm A Rock'
	'Who Are The Brain Police'/'Trouble Comin' Every Day'
	'Motherly Love'/'Ain't Got No Heart'
1967	*'Big Leg Emma'/'Why Don't You Do Me Right'*
	'Son Of Suzy Creamcheese'/'Big Leg Emma'
	'Mother People'/'Lonely Little Girl'
1968	*'Desert'/'Jelly Roll Gum Drop'*
	'My Guitar'/'Dog Breath 1970'/'Peaches En Regalia'/
	'Little Umbrellas'.
	'WLPJ'/'My Guitar'
	'Will You Go All The Way For USA'/'Tell Me You Love Me'
1971	*'What Will This Evening Bring Me This Morning'/*
	'Daddy, Daddy, Daddy'
	'Tears Began To Fall'/'Junior Mintz Boogie
	'Happy Together'/'Tears Began To Fall'
1972	*'Cletus Awreetus Awrightus'/'Eat That Question'*
1973	*'Montana'/'I'm The Slime'*
1974	*'Cosmik Debris'/'Uncle Remus'*
	'Don't Eat The Yellow Snow'/'Camarillo Brillo'
1975	*'Du Bis Mein Sofa'/'Stink Foot'*
1976	*'Find Her Finer'/'Zoot Allures'*
	'Disco Boy'/'Mrs Pinky'
1979	*'Dancin' Fool'/'Baby Snakes'*
	'Joe's Garage'/'Central Scrutinizer'
	'Bobby Brown'/'Baby Snakes'
	'Joe's Garage'/'Catholic Girls'
	'Stick It Out'/'Why Does It Hurt When I Pee?'
	'I Don't Wanna Get Drafted'/'Ancient Armaments'
1981	*'For The Young Sophisticate'/'Love Of My Life'*
	'You Are What You Is'/'Pink Napkins'
	'Harder Than Your Husband'/'Dumb All Over'
	'Goblin Girl'/'Pink Napkins'
1982	*'You Are What You Is'/'Harder Than Your Husband'/*
	'Pink Napkins'/'Soup 'N Old Clothes' (12 inch)
	'Shut Up 'N Play Yer Guitar'/'Variations On The Carlos Santana Secret'/'Why Johnny Can't Read' (12 inch).
	'Valley Girl'/'You Are What You Is' (maxi)
	'Valley Girl'/'Teenage Prostitute'
	'Valley Girl'/'No Not Now'
1984	*'Baby, Take Your Teeth Out'/'Steve's Spanking'*
1985	*'He's So Gay'/'In France'/'Be In My Video'/'Baby Take Your Teeth Out' (maxi).*

33 rpm

1966	FREAK OUT. *US Verve V6 5005*
1967	ABSOLUTELY FREE. *US Verve V6 5013*
1968	WE'RE ONLY IN IT FOR THE MONEY. *US Verve V6 045*
	LUMPY GRAVY. *US Verve V6 8741*
	RUBEN & THE JETS. *US Verve V6 5055*
1969	UNCLE MEAT. *US Bizarre MS 2024*
	HOT RATS. *US Bizarre RS 6356*
	BURNT WEENY SANDWICH. *US Bizarre RS 6370*
1970	WEASELS RIPPED MY FLESH. *US Bizarre RSL P 2028*
	CHUNGA'S REVENGE. *US Bizarre MS 2030*
1971	FILLMORE EAST. *US Bizarre MS 2042*
	200 MOTELS. *US United Artists VAS 9956*
1972	JUST ANOTHER BAND FROM L.A. *US Bizarre MS 2075*
	WAKA JAWAKA. *US Bizarre MS 2094*
	THE GRAND WAZOO. *US Bizarre MS 2093*
1973	OVER NITE SENSATION. *US Discreet MS 2149*
1974	APOSTROPHE. *US Discreet DS 2175*
	ROXY & ELSEWHERE. *US Discreet DS 2202*
1975	ONE SIZE FITS ALL. *US Discreet DS 2216*
	BONGO FURY. *US Discreet DS 2234*
1976	ZOOT ALLURES. *US Warner Bros BS 22970*
1978	IN NEW YORK. *US Discreet 2290*
	STUDIO TAN. *US Discreet DSK 2291*
1979	SLEEP DIRT. *US Discreet 2292*
	SHEIK YERBOUTI. *US Zappa Records SRZ-2-1501*
	ORCHESTRAL FAVORITES. *US Discreet DSK 2294*
	JOE'S GARAGE. ACT. 1. *US Zappa Records SRZ-1-1603*
	JOE'S GARAGE. ACTS II & III. *US Zappa Records SRZ-2-1502*
1981	TINSELTOWN REBELLION. *US Barking Pumpkin Record PW2 32336*
	SHUT UP 'N PLAY YER GUITAR. *US Barking Pumpkin Records BPR 1111/1112/1113*
	YOU ARE WHAT YOU IS. *US Barking Pumpkin Records. PW2 37537*
1982	SHIP ARRIVING TOO LATE TO SAVE THE DROWNING WITCH. *FW 38066*
1983	THE MAN FROM UTOPIA. *FW 38403*
	SOUNDTRACK BABY SNAKES. *Picture disc. BPR 1115*
	THE LONDON SYMPHONY ORCHESTRA. *Zappa, volume 1. FW 38820*
1984	THE PERFECT STRANGER. *D5 38170*
	THEM OR US. *SVBO 742000*
	THINGFISH. *SCKO 74201*
1985	OLD MASTERS. *BPR 7777*
1985	FRANK ZAPPA MEETS THE MOTHERS OF PREVENTION. *ST 74203*
1986	*DOES HUMOR BELONG IN MUSIC? Live. EMI CDP 746188-2.*

N.B. Unlike the annotated discography which gives the dates completed, these lists give the dates released.

Albums Never Released

LUMPY GRAVY (instrumental). While on contract to MGM, Zappa was given the opportunity to do an album with Capitol. It was recorded with the Emuukha Electric Orchestra, in New York but never released. A record with the same title came out, consisting of the same material but with The Mothers' contributions added.

SINK TRAP/GYPSY AIRS. Instrumental single.

OUR MAN IN NIRVANA. Intended for release in 1967. Features Lenny Bruce.

THE HISTORY AND COLLECTED IMPROVISATIONS OF THE MOTHERS OF INVENTION. This was to be a twelve record boxed set, containing material recorded between 1962 and 1969, then it was reduced to ten after 'Weasels Ripped My Flesh' and 'Burnt Weeny Sandwich'. It was further reduced to nine, with the title 'No Commercial Potential'. Zappa tried to sell it by running ads in Playboy. The titles are: 'Before The Beginning', 'The Cucamonga Era', 'Boogie', 'The Merely Entertaining Mothers Of Invention Business Record', 'Soup And Old Clothes', 'The Orange County Lumber Truck', 'The Weasel Music'.

'THE NIGHT OF THE IRON SAUSAGE' (two LPS) came out as a single album instead of a double with different titles under the name 'Zoot Allures'.

LATHER was a source of arguments between Zappa and Warner Bros. This was to contain material from 'Zappa In New York', 'Studio Tan', 'Sleep Dirt', 'Orchestral Favorites' etc, but with different mixes than on the Warner releases, and with a different order.

Zappa played the entire set on American radio and invited those interested to record it. The titles are:

1. 'Regyptian Strut', 'Naval Aviation In Art', 'A Little Green Rosetta', 'Duck Duck Goose', 'Down In The Dew', 'For The Young Sophisticate'.
2. 'Tryin' To Grow A Chin', 'Broken Hearts Are For Assholes', 'The Illinois Enema Bandit'.
3. 'Lemme Take You To The Beach', 'Revised Music For Guitar And Low Budget Orchestra', 'Redunzl'.
4. 'Honey Don't You Want A Man Like Me?', 'The Black Page No 1', 'Big Leg Emma', 'Punky's Whips'.
5. 'Flambay', 'Purple Lagoon'.
6. 'Pedro's Dowry', 'Lather', 'Spider Of Destiny', 'Duke Of Orchestral Prunes'.
7. 'Filthy Habits', 'Titties And Beer', 'One More Time For The World'.
8. 'Greggery Peccary'.

CRUSH ALL BOXES.

All of the material from the 1980 tour was to appear on this album. It later came out in a different form under the names 'Tinseltown Rebellion' and 'You Are What You Is'.

Zappappearances

1962 THE MASTERS. 'Breaktime'/'16 Tons', by Williams, Buff and Zappa.
THE PENGUINS. 'Memories Of El Monte'/'Be Mine', written by Zappa/Collins.
BOBBY JAMESON. 'Gotta Find My Roogalator'.
RON ROMAN. 'Love Is My Life'/'Tell Me', written by Zappa, Roman and Aerni.

1963 BABY RAY AND THE FERN. 'Hows Ya Bird?'/'The World's Greatest Sinner', written by Zappa.
BOP GUY. 'Dear Jeepers'/'Letter From Jeepers', written by Zappa.
BRIAN LORD AND THE MIDNIGHTERS. 'The Big Surfer'/'Not Another One', written by Zappa.
NED AND NELDA. 'Hey Nelda'/'Surf Along', written by Zappa.
HOLLYWOOD PERSUADERS. 'Grunion Run'/'Tijuana Surf', written by Zappa who also plays guitar.
JIM MUSIL COMBO. 'Grunion Run'/'North Beach', written by Zappa.
CONRAD AND THE HURRICANE STRINGS. 'Hurricane'/'Sweet Love', produced by Zappa.

1964 MR. CLEAN. 'Mr Clean'/'Jessie Lee', written and produced by Zappa.
ROTATIONS. 'Heavies'/'The Cruncher', produced by Zappa.
THE HEARTBREAKERS. 'Every Time I See You'/'Craddle Rock', Zappa plays various instruments.

1965 THE CHOCOLATE WATCH BAND. 'Loose Lip Sync Ship'/'Blues Theme', produced by Zappa under the name 'The Fantom' (The Hogs).

1967 BURT WARD. 'Boy Wonder I Love You'/'Orange Coloured Sky', written, produced and conducted by Zappa.
THE ANIMALS. 'The Other Side Of My Life'/'It's All Meat', arranged by Zappa.

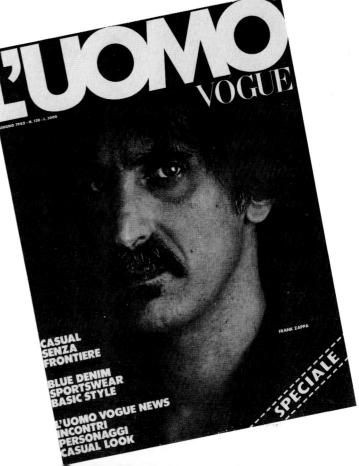

G.T.O.'s: Christine, Mercy Fontenot, Lucy Offerall, Sandra Leano, Sparky Parker, Pamela Miller, Cynderella.

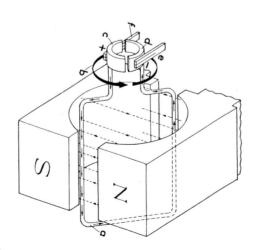

Discography Of Zappa's Contributions To Albums By Others And Cover Versions Of His Material

1966 THE ANIMALS. 'Animalisms'. Zappa arranged 'All Night Long' and 'The Other Side Of My Life'. 4414
1967 THE WEST COAST POP ART EXPERIMENTAL BAND. Cover of 'Help I'm A Rock'. Reprise 6427.
1968 LENNY BRUCE. 'The Berkeley Concert'. Bizarre 6329. Double album produced by Zappa on his label.
WILD MAN FISCHER. 'An Evening With…' Bizarre 6332.
Produced by Zappa.
Percussion by Art Tripp, recitation by Kim Fowley and Rodney Bingenheimer, helped by the GTOs.
1969 DAVE PIKE SET. 'Noisy Silence', MPS 15014. Cover of 'Mother People'.
CAPTAIN BEEFHEART. 'Trout Mask Replica', produced by Zappa (Straight 1053).
LORD BUCKLEY. 'A Most Immaculately Hip Aristocrat', Straight 1054.
Released by Zappa on his label.
FRATERNITY OF MAN. Cover of 'Oh No!', ABC 647.
Produced by Zappa under the name 'Marr Bruister'. He plays on two tracks, and Ian Underwood plays sax.
AMBROSE SLADE. Fontana 5492. Cover of 'I Ain't Got No Heart'.
GTOs. 'Permanent Damage', Straight STS 1059. Produced by Zappa who plays tambourine. The GTOs were a spoof band of groupies. One, Miss Christine, appears on the 'Hot Rats' sleeve and became Alice Cooper's girlfriend. The musicians on this album are Jim Black, Roy Estrada, Ian Underwood, Don Preston, Nicky Hopkins, Jeff Beck and Rod Stewart. Two tracks were written by Davy Jones and Lowell George.
1970 AYNSLEY DUNBAR. 'Blue Whale', BYG 529015. Cover of 'Willie The Pimp'.
JEAN LUC PONTY. 'King Kong', LBS 83375. Written and arranged by Zappa who plays on one track. Other musicians: George Duke, Buell Neidlinger, Art Tripp, Ian Underwood, Wilton Fielder, Ernie Watts and John Guerin.
JUICY LUCY. 'Lie Back', Vertigo 6360014. Cover of 'Willie The Pimp'.
1972 LENNON/ONO. 'Live Jam'. EMI 172 95137/8. On June 6, 1971, John Lennon and Yoko Ono performed during a Mothers' gig at the New York Fillmore. Because of contractual problems, the jam came out on Lennon's label, poorly mixed.
BABE RUTH. 'First Base'. Harvest SHSP 4022. Cover of 'King Kong'.
GOOD GOD. Atlantic 7243, cover of 'King Kong'.

1973 RUBEN AND THE JETS. 'For Real', Mercury ARM 1659. Produced by Zappa who plays guitar on one track, and composed and arranged three songs.
1974 WOODY HERMANN. 'Thundering Herd', Fantasy 9452. Excellent cover of 'America Drinks And Goes Home'.
GEORGE DUKE. 'Feel', MPS 212 2312-4. Zappa plays guitar under the name Obdewl X, which is later found in 'Thingfish'.
1975 GEORGE DUKE. 'The Aura Will Prevail', MPS 68025. Covers of 'Uncle Remus' and 'Edchina'S Arf'.
FLO AND EDDIE. 'Illegal, Immoral And Flattering', CBS 80983. Cover of 'Eddie Are You Kidding?'
1976 GRAND FUNK RAILROAD. 'Good Singin' Good Playin'', produced by Zappa who plays guitar on one track.
1977 GRUPPO SPORTIVO. 'Ten Mistakes', Vogue 20340. Cover of 'Take Your Clothes Off When You Dance' (Zappa), who himself re-used a theme from The Drifters, 'True Love'/'True Love' (Pomus/Shuman).
1978 FLINT. CBS 83297. Ex-members of Grand Funk Railroad, Zappa plays guitar.
ALTERNATIVE TV. 'The Image Has Cracked', Deptford Fun CITY/D1P01. Cover of 'Why Don't You Do Me Right'.
1979 L. SHANKAR. Mercury SRZ 1602. Produced, arranged and orchestrated by Zappa who sings under the name 'Stucco Homes' on 'Dead Girls Of London'.
1980 THE SONICS. 'Unreleased', First American 7719 Goodwin. Cover of 'Any Way The Wind Blows'.
1982 THE GRANDMOTHERS. 'Looking Up Granny's Dress'. Utterly abysmal covers of 'Uncle Meat', 'Mother People', 'Peaches En Regalia', 'Oh No', 'E. Dolphy Memorial Barbecue', 'Go Cry On Somebody Else'. This horrendous album is best avoided.

André Heller's 'Basta' (Intercord 160110) should be added, as it features some of Zappa's best musical accomplices – Peter Wolf, Patrick O'Hearn, Ed Mann, Thomas Nordegg and Ian Underwood – as well as Laurindo Almeida, Airto Moreira and Chaka Khan. Zappa lent them some equipment, notably his emulator. Robert Charlebois' 'Swing' has not been listed because although rumour has it that Zappa played guitar on 'Petroleum', there is no conclusive proof.
1984 FRANCESCO ZAPPA

Groups In Which Zappa Played Prior To The Mothers

THE RAMBLERS
Twelve-year old Zappa played drums in this school band, led by Elwood 'Junior' Mades.
THE BLACKOUTS (or KNOCKOUTS)
A group of eight musicians, three blacks, two Mexicans and three whites which started in 1956 at Antelope Valley High School, Lancaster, California. Zappa left on June 13, 1958.
THE BOOGIE MAN
Formed in Ontario, California, about 1960, and never found a bassist. They practised in Zappa's garage and, apart from Frank on guitar, consisted of Al Surrat (drums), Kenny Burgan (sax) and Doug Rost (guitar).
JOE PERRINO AND THE MELLOW TONES
Played in various bars and clubs in 1962.
THE SOOTS (or OMENS)
Formed in 1963 with three members: Zappa, Don Vliet (later Captain Beefheart) and Alex St. Claire.
THE MUTHERS
Another 1963 band that lasted only briefly as Zappa bought Studio Z. This band played mostly in Mexican clubs around Ontario, and consisted of Zappa (guitar), Les Papp (drums) and Paul Woods (bass).
THE SOUL GIANTS
Zappa met this band in Los Angeles when they were looking for a guitarist. They comprised Roy Estrada (bass), Ray Collins (vocals), Jim Black (drums) and David Coronado (sax).
CAPTAIN GLASSPACK AND HIS MAGIC MUFFLERS
The Soul Giants' new name when Zappa joined. David Coronado left soon after.
THE MOTHERS
The Magic Mufflers adopted this name on Mother's Day 1964.
Their adventures were about to start.

Orchestral Favourites

BICYCLE FOR TWO. In 1963, Zappa and Steve Allen played a concerto for two people on a bicycle.

I WAS A TEENAGE MALTSHOP. In 1963, Zappa recorded some songs for this rock opera (already). As well as the title track, there was 'Status Pack Baby', later on 'Absolutely Free', 'Ned The Mumbler' and 'Ned Has A Brainstrom'. It was turned down by record companies.

In 1963 at Mt. St Mary's College, Claremont Zappa presented a programme of experimental music, followed by a discussion. The pieces played were: 'Piece No. 2 Of Visual Music For Jazz Ensemble And 16mm Visual Projector' (1957), 'Piano Pieces From Opus 5', 'Collage One For String Instruments', 'Opus For Piano, Tape Recorder And Multiple Orchestra', 'Two Fragments Of Prepared Tape For Opus 5'.

CONTEMPO 1970. During this festival of contemporary music at Los Angeles on May 15, 1970, The Mothers and The L.A. Philharmonic Orchestra conducted by Zubin Mehta played orchestral music which already included fragments from '200 Motels'.

ORCHESTRAL FAVORITES. On September 17 and 18, 1975, no less than 37 musicians, who formed the Abnuceals Emuukha Electric Orchestra, conducted by Zappa and Michale Zearott, played electric orchestral music.

NOVA CONVENTION. At this event on December 2, 1978, in the Intermedia Theater, New York, Zappa participated by reading an extract from William Burrough's 'The Talking Asshole'. Other participants included Laurie Anderson, John Cage, Allen Ginsburg, John Giorno, Philip Glass, Brion Gysin, Timothy Leary, Ed Sanders, Patti Smith and Robert Wilson. (2 LPs – Nova Conv. LPS GPS 014 015; Giorno Poetry Systems Rec).

A TRIBUTE TO EDGAR VARÈSE. April 17, 1981. A group of musicians arranged a concert in honour of Varèse. Zappa was asked to present and accepted, but found the hall too small for the occasion, and instead hired the New York Palladium.

LONDON SYMPHONY ORCHESTRA. On January 11, 1983 at the Barbican Theatre, London, after problems arranging it in with the Viennese and Amsterdam Orchestras, Zappa gave a world premier of his symphonic work, conducted by Kent Nogano. Pieces played: 'Envelopes', 'Mo'n'Herb's Vacation', 'Bob In Dacron-Sad Jane', 'Pedro's Dowry' and 'Bogus Pomp'.

SAN FRANSISCO CONTEMPORARY CHAMBER MUSICIANS. In February, 1983, after a first part conducted by Jean Louis Le Roux, Zappa conducted two of Varèse's works, 'Ionisation' and 'Intégrale'.

ENSEMBLE INTERCONTEMPORAIN. At the Théâtre de la Ville, in Paris, on January 9, 1984, Pierre Boulez conducted three of Zappa's pieces for chamber music: 'Dupree's Paradise', 'Naval Aviation In Art' and 'The Perfect Stranger'. For the rest of the evening, works by Charles Ives, Carl Ruggles and Elliott Carter were played.

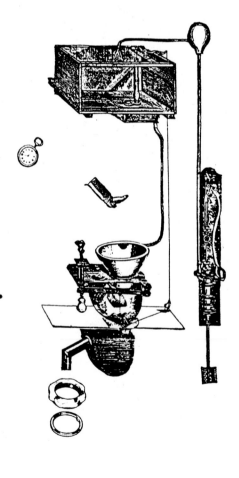

AMERICAN SOCIETY OF UNIVERSITY COMPOSERS, 19TH ANNUAL FESTIVAL. At the University of Columbus, Ohio, on April 4-9, Zappa was invited to this conference and talked about his ideas on music. 'The Black Page' and 'Naval Aviation In Art' were played.

SPEAKING OF MUSIC WITH FRANK ZAPPA. May 20, 1984, Palace of Fine Arts, San Francisco, arranged by Charles Amirkhanian. On the programme: 'Lumpy Gravy' (excerpt, digitally re-mastered), 'Mo'n'Herb's Vacation' (1st Movement), 'Love Story' (synclavier), 'Jonestown' (synclavier) 'Naval Aviation In Art' (Chamber Ensemble), 'Girl In The Magnesium Dress' (synclavier), 'While You Were Out' (guitar version), 'Francesco', Opus 1/6 I/II 1/12 (synclavier), 'Francesco, The Almost Fictional Life Of An Obscure Italian Composer' (text by Zappa, read by Calvin Ahlgreen), 'Francesco Rock Opus I/I' (synclavier), 'He's So Gay' ('Thingfish'), 'Sinister Footwear' and 'Truck Driver Divorce' ('Them Or Us').

A ZAPPA AFFAIR. The Berkeley Symphony Orchestra, Zellerbach Auditorium conducted by Kent Nogano. 'A Zappa Affair' was the world premier of four ballets with giant marionettes, staged on June 15, 1984. Music and scenery by Frank Zappa: 'Bob In Dacron' 'Sad Jane', 'Mo'n'Herb's Vacation', 'Sinister Footwear', 'Pedro's Dowry'.

KRONOS STRING QUARTET. April 12, 1985, San Francisco, consisting of David Harrington and John Sherba (violins), Hank Dutt (alto) and Juan Jeanrenaud (cello) who gave a world premier of a twenty minute piece by Zappa called 'None Of The Above', composed in 1984.

ASPEN WIND QUARTET. Alice Tully Hall, Lincoln Center, New York. This quartet, a 1984 Nuremburg Chamber Music Award winner, played a world premier of Zappa's 'Time's Beach', and consisted of Baili Nugent (flute), Claudia Coonce (oboe), David Krakauer (clarinette), Timothy Ward (bassoon) and Kaitilin Mahony (horn).

Discography Of Compact Discs

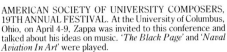

1984 THE PERFECT STRANGER, EMI CDC 7471252
1986 DOES HUMOR BELONG IN MUSIC?. Live, contains previously unreleased material. EMI CDP 7461882.

Zappa has signed a contract with Ryko Disc for 24 compact discs over a period of three years (Billboard 1/2/86). By the end of the summer 1986, eight albums should be available on six CDs: 'Frank Zappa Meets The Mothers Of Prevention', a two-disc version of 'Shut Up 'N' Play Yer Guitar', a single disc featuring both 'Apostrophe' and 'Overnite Sensation' and a collection of Zappa compositions performed by the London Symphony Orchestra, including one previously unreleased piece lasting 27 minutes. Zappa has also signed a three record contract with the Angel label, for compact discs of classico-contemporary music.

VIVA! ŽAPPA